THE
GLENRIDDELL MANUSCRIPTS

THE
GLENRIDDELL MANUSCRIPTS
OF
ROBERT BURNS

WITH AN INTRODUCTION AND NOTES
BY
DESMOND DONALDSON

EP Publishing Limited, Wakefield
Archon Books, Hamden
1973

The facsimile of the Glenriddell Manuscripts is published with the approval of the Trustees of the National Library of Scotland, the owners of the original manuscript.

This edition first published in the United States
by Archon Books, Hamden, Connecticut, 1973,
and in Great Britain by EP Publishing Limited,
1973

ISBN 0 85049 806 2 (EPP)
ISBN 0 208 01323 7 (Archon)

Please address all enquiries to EP Publishing Ltd.
(address as above)

Printed in Great Britain by
Scolar Press Limited, Menston, Yorkshire

CONTENTS

INTRODUCTION

ROBERT BURNS, THE RIDDELL FAMILY AND THE GLENRIDDELL MANUSCRIPTS

When Robert Burns came to Dumfriesshire in 1788 to the farm of Ellisland he was twenty-nine years of age. His reputation as a poet was established, but although his most difficult period of poverty and obscurity was behind him he still had to find a steady income to support his wife and family. Contrary to popular belief Burns had given a great deal of thought to his future; his literary ambitions ran far beyond being a poet and he realized that to bring these ambitions to fruition he needed a good income without being tied down by day-to-day drugery. The farm of Ellisland could, if successful, support a number of workers and would leave the farmer a fair amount of free time, but Burns had another string to his bow; for years past he had had in mind a well paid position in the Excise where little work was involved and regular attendance by no means necessary. To reach this comparatively high position he knew that he would have to start at the bottom as a hard-working gauger and then rely on the influence of highly placed friends to secure his rapid advancement. His first tentative steps towards a position in the Excise seem to have been made in 1786 when in a letter to Robert Aitken, probably written early in October of that year he says: 'I have been feeling all the various rotations and movements within, respecting the Excise . . .'.

The initial efforts of Burns and his friends culminated in his appointment to the Dumfries First Itinerancy in the autumn of 1789, as a part-time Exciseman, and from then on, apart from one or two slips, he continued to advance in the Excise Service and if he had not died in 1796 he would almost certainly have reached the position of Collector at a comparatively early age. When he arrived at Ellisland, therefore, Robert Burns was at a turning point in his career.

Burns' nearest neighbour at Ellisland was Robert Riddell, a country gentleman who lived in a mansion house called Friar's Carse. Robert Riddell (1755–1794) could trace his descent back to Gervase Ridel, a Norman who followed David I from England circa 1225 and who received from the King the appointment of Sheriff of Roxburgh, together with grants of land in the neighbourhood. By the eighteenth century the status of the Riddells had declined somewhat though they were still land-owners (in Dumfriesshire now) and important people locally. In Burns' time two brothers, Robert and Walter, were the heads of the family. Robert Riddell had married Elizabeth Kennedy of Manchester in 1784 and settled in Friar's Carse. In 1788 he inherited Glenriddell, the family seat, but continued to live at Friar's Carse. Walter Riddell had spent some time in Antigua where he owned sugar plantations inherited from his first wife who died in 1787. Walter then married Maria Woodley, also the daughter of a plantation owner, and the couple returned to Scotland in 1791 and settled in Woodley Park only a few miles from Friar's Carse.

Normally, the peasant farmer and the land-owning family would have had little in common. Burns, however, was no ordinary farmer and both Robert Riddell and his sister-in-law Maria, unlike the squirearchy of their day, were deeply interested in the Arts. Robert Riddell welcomed Burns to his house, made him feel at home there, and gave him the freedom of a small Hermitage in the grounds of Friar's Carse where he could meditate and write. Burns and the Riddells were on terms of easy friendship: we hear of the Riddells giving Burns engravings to hang in his parlour and of Burns going to great pains to procure for the Riddells a good Ayrshire cow. Next we find Riddell sending his newspaper across to Ellisland and Burns returning it with the verse:

> 'Your news & review, sir
> I've read through and through, sir,
> With little admiring or blaming. . . .'

Later we find Burns writing as a note to 'The Day Returns':

> "I composed this song out of compliment to one of the happiest and worthiest married couples in the world—Robert Riddell of Glenriddell and his lady. At their fireside I have enjoyed more pleasant evenings than at all the houses of fashionable people in the country: and to their kindness and hospitality I am indebted for many of the happiest hours of my life."

This friendship continued for three years after Robert Burns left Ellisland to take up a full-time position in the Excise at Dumfries until it was broken in 1794 by a most unfortunate episode.

It was from the friendship between Robert Burns and Robert Riddell that the idea came for Burns to compile a special manuscript collection of selected items of his work both in poetry and in prose, which he would present to Robert Riddell. Two quarto volumes of slightly differing size were obtained; they were bound in calf with the Glenriddell arms stamped on the boards and each had an impression of the

Beugo engraving of Burns' head pasted on the frontispiece. One volume was to be reserved for poetry and the other for prose. Burns took a great interest in compiling the two collections. Contrary to the impression he liked to give, Robert Burns usually wrote with an eye to future publication. His letters were not dashed off on the spur of the moment and were rarely mere replies to letters received. They were literary compositions, carefully drafted and corrected and he kept copies of most of them. The task before him was, therefore, one of selection, but in spite of this the work took a long time. The first volume, containing poems, was ready, if we can trust the date of the Preface, by 27th April 1791, but the second volume took much longer and we find Burns writing to Mrs. Dunlop on 25th December 1793:

> "I have lately collected, for a friend's perusal, all my letters: I mean, those which I first sketched in a rough draft, and afterwards wrote out fair. On looking over some old musty papers, which, from time to time, I have parcelled by, as trash that were scarce worth preserving, and which yet at the same time I did not care to destroy, I discovered many of these rude sketches, and have written, and am writing them out, in a bound M.S.S. for my Friend's Library."

This volume of prose was never given to the man for whom it was intended; before it was finished, a regrettable breach between Burns and the Riddell family occurred. The exact cause of this breach is never likely to be known in spite of all the detective work that has been done on it, as there are far too many contradictory clues and unanswered questions. The result, however, is indisputable: Robert Riddell withdrew his friendship, and when Burns tried to apologise to the Riddells he was rebuffed.

Robert Riddell died before any reconciliation could be brought about and Burns wrote to Riddell's relatives (7th May 1794) asking for the return of the book of poems,

> "You know that at the wish of my late friend, I made a collection of all my trifles in verse which I had ever written. There are many of them local, some of them peurile and silly, and all of them unfit for the public eye. As I have some little fame at stake—a fame that I trust may live when the hate of those who 'watch for my halting' and the contumelious sneer of those whom accident has made my superiors, will, with themselves, be gone to the region of oblivion; I am uneasy now for the fate of those manuscripts. Will Mrs. [Riddell] have the goodness to destroy them or return them to me? As a pledge of friendship they were bestowed; and that circumstance, indeed, was all their merit."

The volume was returned to Burns and he made several additions to it, one of them being the cruel epigram against Maria Riddell—"If you rattle along like your mistress's tongue" (see Poems, p. 161).

In spite of the fierceness of the quarrel, reconciliation between Burns and Maria was brought about gradually and by August 1795 they were on good terms again and exchanging letters. When Robert Burns died on 21st July 1796, Maria wrote a short Biographical note which was published in the Dumfries Mercury. It is outstanding for its lack of bias and penetrating analysis of the poet's talent and character.

After Burns' death both volumes of the Glenriddell Manuscripts, as they became known, were among the material which his widow handed over to his biographer, Dr. Currie. This material was never returned to the poet's family and indeed there is no indication that they ever asked for its return. The next news we have of the Glenriddell Manuscripts is that the widow of Mr. Wallace Currie (the son of Dr. Currie) presented them to the Liverpool Athenaeum. On the 6th December 1853, she wrote to the President,

> Sir,—Will you allow me to make you the medium of presenting to the Anthenaeum Library two manuscript books, in his own writing, of Poems and Letters of Burns?
>
> I believe they came into the possession of Dr. Currie when he was engaged in writing the Life of the Poet; and I shall feel gratified by their finding a place in the library of an institution in which he took so great an interest.
>
> I am, Sir,
Your obedient servant,
S. Currie.

There was no thought here of returning them to Burns' relatives, or to any institution in which he (Burns) took an interest.

The Manuscripts were put away in a wooden box and apparently forgotten for twenty years until a Mr. Henry A. Bright 'discovered' them and put them on exhibition. In 1913 the Liverpool Athenaeum decided to sell the Manuscripts and gave Messrs. Sotheby & Co. a six-month option on them at £5,000. When Sothebys exercised the option the matter became public and there was a considerable outcry in Scotland, culminating in an attempt to have the sale cancelled. This attempt was widely supported by prominent people who issued a statement seeking support in November 1913. They were too late, however; the Manuscripts had already left the country and were in the hands of an American dealer. By a great stroke of luck the dealer offered them to John Gribbel of Philadelphia. What happened then is best told in Gribbel's own words. Speaking at the annual meeting of the St. Andrew Society of Philadelphia on 30th November 1913, he said,

> "Two weeks ago, I was astonished beyond measure by having a dealer come to Philadelphia and submit to me for sale the missing manuscripts. Having an aversion to the possession of property of a certain class, I refused to consider them as any possible possession of my own, priceless though they are. But, gentlemen, here they are, sold as merchandise in the market-place, and in my possession, but with a purpose which I am sure you will approve. Very largely influenced by my association with you, these precious writings go to Scotland to stay there for ever and protected by a deed of trust, as a gift to the people who gave the world—Robert Burns."

As a result of this quite exceptional act of generosity the Manuscripts were returned to Scotland and are now lodged in the National Library of Scotland, King George IV Bridge, Edinburgh. Before parting with the Manuscripts John Gribbel had a facsimile reproduction made by the Beck Engraving Company of Philadelphia; only 150 copies were printed and the plates and negatives were then destroyed. This is now a rare and valuable collectors' edition. The present edition is intended to bring these manuscripts before a wider public, thus making them available to students of Burns to whom the Glenriddell Manuscripts are at present only a name.

DUMFRIES COUNTY LIBRARY
MAY 1972

Desmond Donaldson
F.L.A., F.R.S.A., F.S.A.(SCOT.)

DESCRIPTION OF THE ORIGINAL GLENRIDDELL MANUSCRIPTS NOW IN THE NATIONAL LIBRARY OF SCOTLAND

The text of this facsimile is a faithful reproduction of the original but, of course, there are differences in format. The original manuscripts are bound in two volumes which differ in the following particulars from the facsimile:

VOLUME I—POEMS. The frontispiece is exactly as in this facsimile except that the portrait is on a separate piece of paper stuck on the page. The portrait is a print of the Beugo engraving of the Nasmyth portrait, while the remainder of the page is hand done in indian ink. The frontispiece is on the blank inner side of the marbled end paper. The title page is exactly as in this facsimile except that a blue stamp, oval in shape, with the words NATIONAL LIBRARY | OF SCOTLAND | EDINBURGH appears at the foot of the page. The title page is of much flimsier paper than the rest of the volume which, as in the other volume, is in hand-made rag paper. The size of the original is 24 x 18.5 cm. The original volume is bound in calf and the spine has been replaced, but most of the gold decoration from the original spine has been put back. The boards have gilt border decoration different from that in the other volume and the spine is in six boxes. The second box contains a black label with the words BURNS'S | POEMS in gold. The other boxes are heavily gilt with a circular centre ornament in each. In the centre of the front board is the Glenriddell Arms in gold. The end papers are marbled in reds and greens, and the arms of the Riddells, hand drawn and coloured, are on a piece of paper stuck on the end paper covering the inside of the front board. The leather of the boards looks much older and more worn than that of the Letters volume. The letter to the President of the Athenaeum with the envelope which contained it, both with heavy black borders, are pasted on the inside of the rear board. The notes made by Dr. Currie in this volume are in pencil.

VOLUME II—LETTERS. The title page is exactly as in this facsimile except that an oval stamp bearing the words NATIONAL LIBRARY | OF SCOTLAND | EDINBURGH appears at the top centre of the page. The frontispiece is exactly as in this facsimile except that the portrait is obviously a separate piece of paper stuck on the page. The portrait is a print of the Beugo engraving of the Nasmyth portrait, while the remainder of the page is hand done in indian ink. The size of the original is 26.5 x 21 cm. The original volume is bound in calf and the spine has been replaced, but most of the original spine ornament and the entire title label have been put back. The boards have gilt border decoration and the spine is in six boxes, the second containing the title BURNS'S | LETTERS in gold on a red ground. The other boxes are gilt with an urn ornament in the centre of each. This binding is unlike that of the Poems volume and if it is the original the volumes have not been made as a pair. Most of the old accounts say that both volumes have the Glenriddell Arms in gold on the outside of the front boards. The arms do not appear on the boards of the present day binding of the Letters volume and these boards look much fresher and newer than those of the Poems volume. High up on the outside of the front board is a B in ink done by hand. Notes by Currie throughout are in red ink except that on page 99 which is in dark ink.

THE TEXT OF THE GLENRIDDELL MANUSCRIPTS

The Glenriddell manuscripts constitute one of the great treasures of the National Library of Scotland and of the Scottish people. Mostly in Burns' handwriting and all chosen, redrafted and checked by the poet himself, they form the largest single manuscript collection of his works and are priceless.

Probably more than any other great writer Robert Burns has had his works edited, altered, cut, and sometimes even expanded by those who collected them. Beginning with Currie, Burns' early editors and biographers felt free to alter texts and facts to suit the image of Burns they wished to project.

This manuscript collection gives Robert Burns' own text of the items it contains and in many cases the only remaining manuscript version of these texts, which adds greatly to their value.

W H Bartlett.

F. Wallis.

A Contemporary print of Ellisland, where Robert Burns lived.

1   Song.
'In Mauchline there dwells six proper young Belles,'

This poem was written in 1784 or 1785. The 'Young Belles' were Jean Armour 1767–1834. (Robert Burns acknowledged her as his wife in 1788). Helen Miller who later married Burns' surgeon friend John McKenzie. Betty Miller who married a Mauchline man named Templeton and died in 1794. Jean Markland, who married James Finlay, Excise Officer at Tarbolton in 1788. Jean Smith who married James Candlish, a teacher and later medical lecturer in Edinburgh and Christina Morton who married Robert Paterson, a Mauchline draper, in 1788.

1   Song.
'Anna, thy charms my bosom fire,'

This poem was to Anne Stewart who was engaged to Alexander Cunningham, Burns' friend, but jilted him for Forrest Dewar an Edinburgh surgeon. Burns sent this song to Mrs. Dunlop on 12th February 1788.

2   Epistle to John Goldie, in Kilmarnock.
'O Gowdie, terror o' the whigs,'

John Goldie or Gowdie (1717–1809) was a miller's son and a man of ability and advanced opinions to which he was not slow to give expression. He was one of Burns' guarantors for the Kilmarnock edition and published several works himself including *Essays on various important subjects moral and divine*, popularly known as 'Gowdie's Bible'. He opposed the conservative religious opinions of the day and his theories appealed to Burns. This poem shows Burns' admiration for Goldie and is one of his earliest satires on orthodox Calvinism. The Glenriddell MS. provides the only complete text.

4   To Miss Jeany Cruikshank.
'Beauteous Rose-bud, young and gay,'

Miss Jeany Cruikshank was the daughter of William Cruikshank, Classics Master in the Edinburgh High School. Burns lodged in his house, 2 St. James's Square, Edinburgh, in the autumn and winter of 1787, when Jeany would be about twelve years old. Burns corresponded with Cruikshank after he settled in Dumfriesshire.

6   Written in Friar's Carse Hermitage.
'Thou whom chance may hither lead,'

> This is the first version of this poem, the second appears on page 15. It was in all probability the first poem of the Ellisland period.

8   On Captn. Grose's peregrinations through Scotland.
'Hear, Land o' Cakes, and brither Scots,'

> Captain Francis Grose (1731–91), son of a Swiss immigrant, was a man of varied achievements. He was in the army for a time and later became interested in art and secured the position of Richmond Herald. He gave up this position and took to writing on antiquarian subjects. He produced the *Antiquities of England and Wales* 6v. 1773–87 and the *Antiquities of Scotland* 2v. 1789–91. He died in Ireland while gathering more antiquarian material. He was a jovial man and he and the poet Burns took to each other immediately. They met at the Riddells' house while Grose was collecting material for his *Antiquities of Scotland*.

11   Ode to the departed Regency-bill, 1789.
'Daughter of Chaos' doting years,'

> Burns called this poem a 'political Squib' and said 'Politics is dangerous ground for me to tread on, and yet I cannot for the soul of me resist an impulse of anything like Wit' (letter to Mrs. Dunlop, 3rd April 1789, with earliest version of the poem). The Glenriddell MS. is the final version. When George III became insane in November 1788, the question of the appointment of a Regent arose. The usual political manoeuvring followed, when suddenly the King regained his sanity (Feb. 1789).

19   Song Tune, Banks of Banna.
'Yestreen I had a pint o' wine,'

> Burns described this as 'I think [it] is the best love-song I ever composed in my life; but in its original state, is not quite a lady's song' (letter to Thomson, 7th April 1793). The original state is probably that represented in the Glenriddell MS. The song was probably written in 1790; and Anna was Anne Park, niece of the landlady of the Globe Tavern, Dumfries. Very little is known about Anne, except that she had a daughter Elizabeth to Burns only nine days before Jean Armour presented him with a son, William Nicol (31st March 1791).

21   Holy Willie's Prayer.
      'O thou that in the heavens does dwell!'

Holy Willie—William Fisher (1737–1809) was a farmer at Mauchline and an elder of that parish. The poem was written early in 1785 and in his letter to Doctor Moore, Burns says '[it] alarmed the Kirk Session so much, that they held three several meetings to look over their holy artillery if any of it was pointed against prophane Rhymes. Unluckily for me, my idle wanderings led me, on another side, point-blank within the reach of their heaviest metal (p. 44)'. This poem was never published in Burns' lifetime, appearing first in 1799. The power of this poem is well expressed by Snyder (pp. 160–161)—'Again, superlatives are needless; yet one can hardly resist saying that this poem alone would have admitted Burns to the fellowship of Swift and Aristophanes. Indeed, one is hard put to it to find anywhere in literature another hundred lines of satiric verse which can rank with it. Here is the merciless pillorying of a specific individual, and of an individual as well known in his community as was Euripides in the Athens that delighted in *The Frogs*. Here is the devastating attack upon the general system of belief which that individual represented; here is the artistic restraint which kept the portrait of William Fisher from becoming a mere caricature, and hence from losing its significance as satire. Here is the brilliant phrase, the flawless rhythm, and—burning through every line—the saeva indignatio which only genius can impart to the printed page.'

26   Epigram—On Captn. F. Grose—Antiquarian.
      'The Devil got notice that Grose was adying.'

Another fruit of the friendship between the Riddells, Burns and Grose. Captain Grose's extreme corpulence was a matter of fun between himself and his friends.

27   Copy of Letter from Mr. Burns to Doctor Moor.

Dr. John Moore (1729–1802). Born at Stirling, he studied medicine at Glasgow University and later served in the Low Countries as surgeon's mate. He continued his studies in Paris, where he became surgeon to the British Ambassador and later was doctor and travelling companion to two successive Dukes of Hamilton. He settled in London in 1778 as a medical practitioner and also became well known as an author, producing *View of Society and Manners in France, Switzerland and Germany*, 2v. 1779. This was followed by other travel books and by a very popular first novel *Zeluco*, 1786. In 1792 he was in Paris and witnessed the uprising there. On his return he wrote *A Journal During a Residence in France*

27 and *A view of the causes and progress of the French Revolution*. He died in London.

It was Mrs. Dunlop who aroused Moore's interest in Burns. A correspondence sprung up between Burns and Moore, the main item of which was the famous Autobiographical Letter written on 2nd August 1787 in Mauchline, followed by a letter from Ellisland on 4th January 1789, which brought the story up to date. On Moore's side the letters contained advice to Burns to write in standard English, advice which he wisely ignored. Burns had a high opinion of Dr. Moore, but disagreed with him over his opinions on the French Revolution and their correspondence ceased.

This autobiographical letter has been a mine of information to Burns' biographers.

49 Tam o'Shanter—A Tale.
'When chapman billies leave the street,'

When Burns met Captain Grose at Friar's Carse (see note on poem 6, p. 8) he asked Grose, who was compiling his *Antiquities of Scotland*, to include a drawing of Alloway-Kirk in his collection, as this was the burial-place of Burns' father. Grose agreed on condition that Burns write a witch-story to be printed along with it. The result was *Tam o' Shanter*. The poem was published in the second volume of the *Antiquities* in April 1791, having been printed earlier in the *Edinburgh Magazine* for March 1791. 'Tam' is by general consent one of the greatest narrative poems in the language. Burns himself described this poem as his 'standard performance in the Poetical line' displaying 'a force of genius & finishing polish that I despair of ever excelling'. This version contains the four additional lines beginning 'Three Lawyers tongues. . . .'.

60 On the death of Sir James Hunter Blair.
'The lamp of day with ill-presaging glare',

Sir James Hunter Blair (1741–1787) was born James Hunter, in Ayr and after succeeding as a banker in Edinburgh he bought the Ayrshire estate of Robertland about 1774. He married the daughter of John Blair of Dunskey, heiress to a considerable fortune, in 1770, and added Blair to his name. He was M.P. for Edinburgh 1780–1784 and Lord Provost of Edinburgh in 1784. He was created a Baronet in 1786 and in that year acquired the estate of Whitefoord. He died on 1st July 1787. The holograph note in this MS. shows Burns' feeling for him although the poem is poor. (Burns describes it as 'but mediocre' and Ferguson describes it as 'the disastrous Elegy on the death of Sir James Hunter Blair'.)

63   Written on the blank leaf of a Copy of the first Edition of my Poems . . .
'Once fondly lov'd, and still remember'd dear,'

> The girl here is Margaret Thomson. Burns met her in Kirkoswald, and in
> the Autobiographical Letter (p. 39) refers to her as 'a charming Fillette
> who lived next door to the school, over-set my Trigonometry, and set me
> off in a Tangent from the sphere of my studies'. Peggy Thomson married
> John Neilson of Monnyfee in 1784.

64   On reading in a Newspaper the death of J. McLeod . . .
'Sad thy tale thou idle page',

> This poem refers to John McLeod of Raasay who died in 1787. Burns
> met him in Edinburgh shortly before his death. The sister referred to by
> Burns was Isabella McLeod to whom he sent this poem from Mossgiel.
> He also wrote two poems for Isabella—*Raving winds around her blow-
> ing* and *To Miss Isabella McLeod*. It is an interesting point that the
> father of John and Isabella McLeod was the Laird of Raasay who
> entertained Dr. Johnson at Raasay House in 1773.

66   Epitaph on a Friend.
'An honest man here lies at rest',

> This poem refers to William Muir (1745–93) who was a miller in Tar-
> bolton. He was a friend of the Burns family and gave Jean Armour shelter
> during her estrangement from her family in March 1788. When Muir
> died, Burns reciprocated his kindness by helping his widow. This poem
> appears in the First Commonplace Book where the first line is—'Here
> lies a cheerful, honest breast'.

67   The humble petition of Bruar Water to the Noble Duke of Athole.
'My Lord, I know your noble ear,'

> This was one of the poems written by Burns as recompense for hos-
> pitality received. Of this one he said 'It eases my heart a good de[al, as
> R]hyme is the coin with which a Poet pays his debts of honor or grati-
> tude' (to Josiah Walker, 5th Sept., 1787). The poem was written at the
> beginning of September 1787 when he stayed at Blair for several days
> during his Highland Tour with Nicol. The Duke is reported to have been
> pleased with it. This was an important visit for Burns as he met several
> people who were to be of use to him later, including Robert Graham of
> Fintry.

72   Extempore Epistle to Mr. McAdam . . .
'Sir, o'er a gill I got your card,'

> John McAdam (d. 1790) of Craigengillan, south of Mauchline, was a rich landowner and agricultural improver who showed an interest in Burns. It seems likely that this poem was written in Edinburgh early in 1787, which would mean that Burns' parenthesis in the title is a mistake.

74   On scaring some Water fowl in Loch Turit
'Why ye tenants of the lake,'

> Sir William Murray of Ochtertyre (d. 1800). Burns first met him at Blair Athol in September 1787, during his Highland tour. A short time after, he visited Murray at Ochtertyre in Strathearn during his tour in Clackmananshire with Doctor Adair, and it was during this stay that the poem was written. Sir William was a cousin of Robert Graham of Fintry.

77   Written in the Hermitage at Taymouth.
'Admiring Nature in her wildest grace,'

> This poem was written by Burns during his Highland tour, probably on 29th August 1787. It was first printed in the Edinburgh *Evening Courant* for 6th September 1787, where it was stated to be contributed by 'O. B. Kenmore Sept 1' who 'a few days ago, being on a visit to Taymouth, . . . found the following verses (by the celebrated Ayrshire bard) written on the walls of the Hermitage there'. O. B. was probably Burns himself.

79   Written at the Fall of Foyers.
'Among the heathy hills and ragged woods,'

> This poem was written on Wednesday 5th September 1787 when Burns came down Loch Ness to Foyers during his Highland tour.

80   Written by somebody on the window of an inn at Stirling . . .
'Here Stewarts once in triumph reign'd,'

> This poem was written at Stirling, probably on 27th August 1787. The Rev. George Hamilton of Gladsmuir answered Burns in verses which were published in *Animadversions on some Poets . . . especially R—t B—s . . .* By James Maxwell, Poet in Paisley, 1788.

81   Epistle to Robt. Graham Esq. of Fintry . . .
          'Fintry, my stay in wordly strife,'

Robert Graham (1749–1815). He was the son of a country gentleman and at the age of seven inherited his father's estates. He was given a good education and when he was fourteen years of age he went to the University of St. Andrews. Robert Graham came of age in 1770 and entered into full possession of the family estates and the following year he became factor to the Earl of Strathmore and to Archibald Douglas of Douglas for all their lands in the Counties of Forfar and Perth. He married Margaret Elizabeth Mylne, who was his second cousin, on 12th April 1773. Graham never seems to have been in a sound condition financially and in 1785 he granted a trust disposition to his whole estate in favour of Alexander Farquharson, accountant in Edinburgh. The estate was to be sold to pay Graham's debts. It was a condition of the sale that the name of the estate was to revert to Linlathan, while Graham was to continue to hold the territorial designation 'of Fintry'. It was in 1787 that Robert Graham received the appointment which brought him into touch with Robert Burns; in that year he was appointed one of the Commissioners of Excise in Scotland. In the autumn of the same year Graham and Burns met for the first time at Blair Castle, the home of the Duke and Duchess of Atholl, when Burns was on his Highland tour with William Nicol as his travelling companion. The correspondence between Burns and Graham began with a letter written by Burns from Edinburgh in January of 1788 (see *Burns Chronicle* Vol. 6 Second Series, 1931, p. 51 for list of letters). Burns came to rely on Graham as his main patron especially after the death of the Earl of Glencairn. Robert Graham died at Balgowan where he appears to have resided after the sale of his estates. The original MS. of this poem sent to Graham of Fintry is dated 10th June 1790. Burns took a great interest in the 1790 election of a Parliamentary representative for the Dumfries Burghs (Dumfries, Lochmaben, Annan, Kirkcudbright and Sanquhar) and wrote several ballads for the campaign, which commenced in September 1789. Contrary to what might have been expected Burns supported the Tory candidate Sir James Johnstone of Westerhall against the Whig Captain Miller, who was the son of Patrick Miller, Burns' landlord. The main reason for this seems to have been his dislike of the leader of the Whig side, the Duke of Queensberry.

87   A Poet's welcome to his love-begotten daughter . . .
          'Thou's welcome, Wean! Mischanter fa' me,'

Elizabeth Paton was a servant girl in the Burns' house at Lochlea. She bore him a child on 22nd May 1785. Burns' mother wanted him to marry Elizabeth Paton; his brother, however, was against the idea and Robert himself seems never to have had any intention of doing so. The child, 'Dear bought Bess' was also named Elizabeth and was brought up at

87   Mossgiel by Burns' mother. When Robert Burns died she returned to her own mother who was by this time married. When Elizabeth reached the age of twenty-one she received two hundred pounds from the fund raised for the support of Burns' family. She married John Bishop and died on 8th January 1817.

89   The five Carlins—A Ballad.
      'There was five Carlins in the South,'

      This is one of the better ballads composed for the 1790 Election (see Notes p. (23)).

104   On the birth of Monsr. Henri, posthumous child . . .
      'Sweet Floweret, pledge o' meikle love,'

      James Henri, referred to in the note to this poem, was the husband of Mrs. Dunlop's daughter Susan and tenant of Loudoun Castle. He died on 22nd June 1790 and a son was born to his widow on 15th November. Burns' friendship with the Henris arose from the fact that Mrs. Henri's mother was Mrs. Dunlop, the great friend and correspondent of the poet.

106   Birthday Ode—31st Decem^r. 1787.
      'Afar th' illustrious Exile roams,'

      Like many other Scots Robert Burns was by sentiment a Jacobite but in practice an upholder of the reigning house. He always declared a sentimental attachment to the Stewarts and at times, leaving caution aside, expressed his contempt for the House of Hanover.

109   Ode sacred to the memory of Mrs. Oswald of Auchencrui.
      'Dweller in yon dungeon dark,'

      Mrs. Mary Oswald was the subject of this savage satire. Her husband, a London merchant, bought the Ayrshire estate of Auchencruive in 1764. His wife died in London in 1788 and her body was brought to Ayrshire for burial. Burns had taken shelter from a storm in an inn at Sanquhar when he was turned out by 'the funeral pageantry of the late, great Mrs. Oswald'. He journeyed on to New Cumnock where he wrote the Ode.

111   Extempore—to Mr. Gavin Hamilton.
'To you, Sir, this summons I've sent,'

Gavin Hamilton (1751–1805) was Robert Burns' landlord, patron and friend. He lived in Mauchline where he was born, and practised law there. He became landlord to Robert and Gilbert Burns in 1784 when they took the farm of Mossgiel. Burns and Hamilton became firm friends and Burns dedicated the Kilmarnock volume to him.

114   Lament of Mary Queen of Scots.
'Now Nature hangs her mantle green,'

This poem completed on 6th June 1790 was sent to Mrs. Dunlop, who like Burns had a romantic affection for Mary Queen of Scots.

118   Epistle to Robt. Graham Esqr. of Fintry.
'When Nature her great Masterpiece designed,

125   From Clarinda on Mr. B—'s saying that he had "nothing else to do".
'When first you saw Clarinda's charms,'

Clarinda was Agnes Craig (1759–1841), the daughter of a Glasgow surgeon. She fell in love and married, against the wishes of her family, a young Glasgow lawyer, James M'Lehose. They had four children, but the marriage was unhappy and she left her husband and returned to her father in 1780. In 1782, her father died and Mrs. M'Lehose removed to Edinburgh to a small house in Potter Row. She lived on an annuity and also had help from her uncle, Lord Craig, a Court of Session judge. She met Burns in Edinburgh on 4th December 1787 and a love affair developed between them. When Burns left Edinburgh, his passion for Nancy cooled and she charged him with 'perfidious treachery'. By 1790, however, they were corresponding again and on 6th December 1791 they met in Edinburgh for the last time. On the 27th of that month Burns sent Nancy his poem *Ae Fond Kiss* from Dumfries. This is one of the world's great love poems. In January 1792, Mrs. M'Lehose sailed for Jamaica to join her husband. The reunion was not a success and she returned to Scotland three months later. She never resumed her intimacy with Burns but in her Journal on 6th December 1831 she wrote 'This day I can never forget. Parted with Burns in the year 1791, never more to meet in this world. Oh, may we meet in Heaven!'

129   On the death of the late Lord President Dundas.
'Lone on the bleaky hills, the straying flocks,'

Robert Dundas, Lord Arniston (1713–1787). He became Lord Advocate in 1754 and Lord President of the Court of Session in 1760. Sometimes known as 'the King of Scotland', he held a position of great power.

129   Robert Burns just missed meeting him at Blair during his Highland tour, a meeting which if it had taken place might have altered Burns' whole career for the better. This poem, as Burns admitted, is not a good effort. He said "These kind of subjects are much hackneyed; and besides, the wailings of the rhyming tribe over the ashes of the Great, are damnably suspicious, and out of all character for sincerity." If the poem was unfortunate, its reception was even more so and on this subject Burns says "I wrote a letter, which however was in my very best manner, and inclosing my Poem, Mr. Wood carried all together to Mr. Solicitor Dundas that then was, and not finding him at home, left the parcel for him.—His Solicitorship never took the smallest notice of the Letter, the Poem or the Poet.—From that time, highly as I respect the talents of their Family, I never see the name, Dundas, in a column of a newspaper but my heart seems straitened for room in my bosom . . ." (Letter to Alexander Cunningham, 11th March 1791).

131   The Whistle—A Ballad.
'I sing of a whistle, a whistle of worth,'

    This poem was written to commemorate a drinking contest held at Friar's Carse on the evening of Friday, 16th October 1789. The prize was a small ebony whistle which legend said had been won by one of the Lawrie family from a giant Dane who accompanied Anne, James VI's Danish queen. The whistle was laid on the table at the beginning of the contest and the last contestant to remain sober enough to blow it was the winner and kept the whistle. After a series of contests the whistle passed to the Riddells and on this occasion the contestants were Sir Robert Lawrie, Robert Riddell and Alexander Fergusson of Craigdarroch. John McMurdo of Drumlanrig was the judge and Craigdarroch, who consumed six bottles of claret, the winner.

136   A new Psalm for the Chapel of Kilmarnock.
'O, sing a new song to the L—!'

    This poem was composed on George III's recovery from madness in the spring of 1789. Burns sent the poem to the editor of the London *Star*. It is a parody of the *Presbyterian Metrical Psalter*.

139   A Ballad—On the heresy of Dr. McGill in Ayr.
'Orthodox, Orthodox, wha believe in John Knox,'

    Here we have another example of Burns defending the unorthodox in religion, and it is in his best satirical vein. He composed the poem in the

139   autumn of 1789 but because he was awaiting active duty in the Excise he cautioned his friends not to let it become public and the entire poem does not seem to have been published until it appeared in Cunningham. The event that prompted the poem is as follows. Doctor William M'Gill, one of the two ministers of Ayr, was accused of heresy. He had been ordained in Ayr in 1761 and had been a friend of the poet's father and had helped to shape the religious beliefs of the family. Robert approved of his 'new light' doctrines and had praised him in the *Two Herds*. When Doctor M'Gill published his *Practical Essay on the Death of Jesus Christ*, Edinburgh, 1786, both the book and its author were denounced. In April 1789, the case came before the Presbytery of Ayr and went on to the General Assembly. M'Gill however made a qualified recantation in April 1790 and the case was dropped.

143   To Robt. Graham Esq. of Fintry on receiving a favor.
'I call no goddess to inspire my strains,'

In January 1788, Burns enlisted the help of Robert Graham of Fintry, a Commissioner of the Scottish Board of Excise, to secure for him the appointment of Exciseman, but there were many regulations to be observed and it was August 1789 before Burns actually received an appointment in the Dumfries Division of the Excise, and this poem is his thanks to Graham of Fintry.

150   Lament for James Earl of Glencairn.
'The wind blew hallow frae the hills,'

James Cunningham, Fourteenth Earl of Glencairn (1749–1791). Burns called him 'the Patron from whom all my fame and good fortune took its rise.' He became Burns' patron in Edinburgh, introduced him to Creech and gathered subscribers for the Edinburgh Edition including the entire Caledonian Hunt. He helped Burns with his post in the Excise and generally gained his admiration and gratitude.

154   Epistle to Robert Graham Esq. of Fintry.
'Late crippled of an arm, and now a leg,'

Robert Graham (1749–1815) was the Laird of Fintry in Forfarshire. (See Notes p. (23).) This poem was constructed from various pieces written earlier and the beginning and the end, addressed to Graham, were grafted on. It was sent to Graham on 6th October 1791 when Burns wrote 'Along with two other Pieces, I inclose you a sheetful

154 of groans, wrung from me in my elbow chair, with one unlucky leg on a stool before me.—I will make no apology for addressing it to you: I have no longer a choice of Patrons: the truly noble Glencairn is no more!'

156 Lines to Sir John Whitefoord of Whitefoord, with the poem to the memory of Lord Glencairn.

Sir John Whitefoord (1734–1803). Third Baronet of Blairquhan. He inherited the estate of Ballochmyle but was forced to sell it in 1788 when he incurred heavy losses in the collapse of Douglas, Heron & Co.'s Bank. Whitefoord, however, was by no means poor after this and went to live in Edinburgh. When Burns went to Edinburgh in 1786 he wrote to Whitefoord asking for advice and it was Whitefoord who advised him to press ahead with a second Edition of his poems and to use the proceeds for the stocking of a small farm. Later Burns visited the Whitefoords in Edinburgh and became friendly with various members of the family. The *Lines to Sir John Whitefoord of Whitefoord* were sent to him together with the poem *To the Memory of Lord Glencairn*.

These Epigrams were added after the return of the Manuscript by the Riddell Family.

160 Miss Davies—This poem refers to Miss Deborah Davies. Said by Burns to be 'positively the least creature ever I saw, to be at the same time unexceptionably, and indeed uncommonly, handsome and beautiful; and besides has the felicity to be a peculiar toast of mine.'

160 Dr. Babington was an Episcopalian minister in Dumfries.

160 This poem refers to a William Riddick and was sent to Maria Riddell in October 1793.

161 Refers to Mrs. Walter Riddell (Maria) and, of course, was added after the MS. was returned to Burns.

162 John Bushby was Sheriff Clerk of Dumfries.

162   John Morine bought Ellisland when Burns left. Burns felt aggrieved by Morine's treatment of him at that time.

162   David Maxwell of Cardoness near Gatehouse-of-Fleet.

W.H. Bartlett.

J.T. Wilmore.

A Contemporary print of Friar's Carse, where Robert Riddell of Glenriddell lived.

1–6   There is no known explanation of why the first six pages were left blank.

7   To William Nicol (Carlisle, 1st June 1787).

William Nicol (1744–97). He was the son of a tailor and was born in Annan Parish, Dumfriesshire. Nicol attended Annan School and Edinburgh University where he studied for the ministry but later transferred to medicine. In 1774 he became Classical Master at Edinburgh High School, a position he held until 1795 when he opened a school of his own which he ran until his death in 1797. Nicol was 15 years older than Burns and although he was somewhat pedantic and ill-natured they were great friends. William Nicol had a fondness for drinking and good company and was a radical in politics and religion; he accompanied Burns on his second journey through the Highlands. An example of Nicol's letters to Burns can be seen on page 91 of the volume of letters.

Here Burns tries his hand at a letter in broad Scots with great effect and the reader is left wondering if he should have resisted English models in letter writing as he did in poetry. This letter was written during Burns' first holiday tour with Bob Ainslie as companion (5th May–9th June 1787).

10   To John Arnot of Dalquhatswood in Ayrshire (April 1786).

John Arnot (c. 1730–c. 1789) is a shadowy figure; little is known about the man himself although Maurice Lindsay has unearthed some interesting facts regarding his family. Although Burns obviously had a high regard for this man he mentions him only in this one letter. It is obvious from the letter that something went wrong with John Arnot's affairs, but nothing is known of this.

This is the only surviving MS. of this letter. The reference to the fact that after losing Jean Armour, Burns was looking 'for another wife' is taken to refer to Mary Campbell.

18   To Charles Sharpe of Hoddam (Dumfries, 22nd April 1791).

Charles Sharpe (1750–1813). Originally known as Charles Kirkpatrick, he assumed the surname Sharpe to conform with the conditions in the will of one Matthew Sharpe and so inherited the estate and castle of Hoddam in Dumfriesshire in 1769. He was trained as a lawyer but did not

18 practise, and he was well known locally as a violinist and composer of verse. Burns was friendly with him in his later years and this letter is thought to have been the beginning of the friendship. Sharpe's second son was the well-known Charles Kirkpatrick Sharpe, a man of considerable literary and artistic ability, who remembered meeting Burns when he was a boy and has left us an interesting account of the poet, and a scathing description of Maria Riddell. His eldest son was the General Matthew Sharpe who, after losing a heated argument with one of his tenant farmers had him ejected the following Whitsunday. The tenant was none other than Thomas Carlyle.

The fictitious signature was 'Johnie Faa'. The celebrated Johnnie Faa was the 'Lord & Earl of Little Egypt' (i.e. leader of the gypsies) who terrorised South West Scotland in the seventeenth century: The *Ballad of Johnie Faa* was well known to Burns.

22   To Alexander Cunningham (Ellisland, 24th January 1789).

Alexander Cunningham (c. 1763–1812) was born in Edinburgh. He began a law apprenticeship there in 1774 and after qualifying practised as a lawyer in the capital until 1797, when he retired from the law and set up in a jeweller's business. He was made a Burgess of Edinburgh in 1798 and was a respected and well-liked citizen. When Burns died, Cunningham was the originator of the fund to aid his wife and family, and it was Cunningham who proposed the posthumous collection of Burns' writings to raise money. Cunningham seems to have met Burns during his first Edinburgh period, but the date or circumstances of the meeting are not known. The two, however, became firm friends and kept up a correspondence until the poet's death.

This letter refers to a Miss Anne Stewart whom Cunningham hoped to marry; she jilted him, however, and married Forrest Dewar, an Edinburgh surgeon on 13th January 1789. The letter as it stands here seems singularly unlikely to afford consolation to a jilted lover and Burns, himself, in the final paragraph of the original letter admits as much:—'I intended to go on with some kind of consolatory epistle, when, unawares I flew off in this rhapsodical tangent.—Instead of attempting to resume a subject for which I am so ill-qualified, I shall ask your opinion of some verses I have lately begun . . .' (see Ferguson v. 1. p. 298).

24   To Mrs. Stewart of Stair (September 1786).

Mrs. Catharine Gordon Stewart (d. 1818) was the daughter and heiress of Thomas Gordon of Afton and Stair and wife of Major-General Stewart, M.P.

24 This letter was written to Mrs. Stewart in the autumn of 1786, and from the words 'shall ever with grateful pleasure remember the reception I got when I had the honour of waiting on you at Stair', we can assume that he met the lady for the first time earlier that year. This is the only letter we have from Burns to Mrs. Stewart, but it seems likely that there were others. We know that their friendship continued, for in 1791 he presented her with a volume of fifty-four quarto pages entirely in his holograph containing fourteen of his poems and inscribing it 'To Mrs. General Stewart of Afton—The first person of her sex & rank that patronised his humble lays, this manuscript collection of Poems is presented, with the sincerest emotions of grateful respect, by THE AUTHOR.' This volume is now in the museum at the poet's birthplace at Alloway and is known as the 'Afton Burns Manuscript.' The letter in the Glenriddell MS. accompanied another gift by Burns to Mrs. Stewart of the manuscripts of eight poems written on ten quarto leaves. This collection is now known as 'The Stair Burns Manuscript', to distinguish it from the other, and is also in the Burns' Cottage Museum, Alloway. This letter also appears in Currie, 1800. There is one passage in Currie which does not appear in the Glenriddell MS. and ten words in Currie which appear at the end of the Glenriddell MS. in Currie's handwriting. This suggests that Currie had another source for the letter and Ferguson is of the opinion that Currie may have found these passages in the original draft from which the Glenriddell transcript was made. This may have come into his possession along with other material from Burns' desk. This is the only surviving MS. of this letter.

26 To Miss Wilhelmina Alexander of Ballochmyle (Mossgiel, 18th November 1786).

Wilhelmina Alexander (1756–1843) was aged thirty when she received this letter with its accompanying poem. She was the daughter of a land-owner and the sister of Claud Alexander who bought the estate of Balloch-myle from the Whitefoords (see Notes p. (23)). Burns had seen her while out walking and composed *The Bonnie Lass of Ballochmyle* in her honour. He sent her this letter along with the poem, but Miss Alexander took no notice of either the poet or his poem, and Burns, ever ready to resent a slight, took his revenge in his annotation to this letter. Miss Alexander never married and it is said that she eventually came to regard the poem and the letter as her most treasured possessions.

29 To John McMurdo (Ellisland, 9th January 1789).

John McMurdo (1743–1803). He was factor to the Duke of Queensberry at Drumlanrig, and therefore a man of considerable importance locally. His wife was the daughter of David Blair, Provost of Dumfries (1782–83

29   and 1790–92); they had a large family of seven sons and seven daughters. Burns and McMurdo were firm friends and John McMurdo became one of the trustees of the fund raised to help the poet's family after his death.

The original letter differs in numerous small particulars from the Glenriddell transcript and has the following paragraph at the end, "With, not the Compliments, but the best wishes, the sincerest prayers of the Season for you, that you may see many and happy years with Mrs. McMurdo and your family—two blessings, by the by, to which your rank does not by any means entitle you; a loving wife and fine family being almost the only good things of this life to which the Farm-house and Cottage have an exclusive right." (See Ferguson v. 1. p. 297.)

31   Robert Burns' *First Commonplace Book* was begun in 1783 and terminated abruptly in October 1785. It contains poems, songs, reflections on life, and a number of comments which show the awakening of an interest in Scottish song which was to last all Burns' life. The version given here is much reduced.

On page 33 of the Letters volume Burns mentions 'That judicious philosopher Mr. Smith'. This is, of course, Adam Smith. Burns admired his work and Smith returned his admiration. It is interesting to compare Burns' estimate of Adam Smith with that of Lord Monboddo the famous Court of Session Judge, who befriended Burns in Edinburgh. In 1778 Monboddo said "Smith . . . wrote a foolish book upon morals, and has now published a book upon trade, from the style of which one would think that he had never read any of the writers of Greece or Rome" (Boswell's *Journal* 2nd March 1778).

43   To The Right Honourable William Pitt on Scottish Distillers (1st February 1789.)

William Pitt (1759–1806). The famous Prime Minister. He was made P.M. in December 1783 at the age of 24 and when Burns wrote this letter he seemed likely to fall from office because of the dispute over the Regency Bill.

This open letter to the Prime Minister first appeared in the Edinburgh *Evening Courant*, Mon., 9th February 1789). Burns here comes vigorously to the defence of the Scottish Distillers and indirectly supports the farming community.

48   To Miss Jean McMurdo (Dumfries, July 1793).

Jean McMurdo (1777–1839), eldest daughter of John McMurdo (see Notes p. (33)) was sixteen when she received this rather ponderous letter

(34)

48   along with the song *There was a lass and she was fair*. Burns sent the song to Thomson in 1793 along with an air which had come from Mrs. Burns. Unfortunately Burns asked Thomson to return the air if he did not like it, which Thomson did, and so the tune was lost.

This is the only known MS. form for this letter, though Ferguson says that another transcript was sold at Sotheby's on 19th March 1930.

51   To the Earl of Glencairn (Lawnmarket, Edinburgh, 13th January 1787).

James Cunningham, fourteenth Earl of Glencairn (1749–1791). He was ten years older than the poet and had much the same attitude towards politics and religion as Burns had. Glencairn was open in his admiration for Burns and the admiration was returned in full measure. The poet called him "the Patron from whom all my fame and good fortune took its rise". When Burns was leaving Edinburgh he wrote to the Earl thanking him "for all that patronage, that benevolence, and that friendship with which you have honoured me". In January 1788 he asked the Earl's aid in securing an Excise appointment. Although it is difficult to estimate the full extent of Glencairn's aid to Burns, he was probably not over-stating his debt when he wrote to Alexander Dalziel, "God knows what I have suffered, at the loss of my best Friend, my first my dearest Patron & Benefactor; the man to whom I owe all that I am & have! I am gone into mourning for him; & with more sincerity of grief than I fear some will, who by Nature's ties ought to feel on the occasion." (See Ferguson, v. 2. p. 62.)

This letter has an exaggerated tone of admiration and even fawning, but there is no doubt that Burns had a very high regard for the Earl which may have amounted to hero worship.

53   To Crauford Tait (Ellisland, 15th October 1790).

Crauford Tait (1765?–1832). He was a Writer to the Signet in Edinburgh and succeeded to the Harvieston Estate, Clackmannanshire, in 1800 on the death of his father, John Tait, who entertained Burns in Harvieston in October 1787, when he returned there to court Peggy Chalmers. Apart from what Burns tells us in this letter nothing is known of William Duncan.

56   To Miss Helen Craik (Ellisland, 9th August 1790).

Helen Craik (1750?–1824). At the time of this letter Miss Craik would be aged about forty years. She was the spinster daughter of the well-known Dumfriesshire landowning family of Craik of Arbigland and she lived in

56   the family home about twenty miles from Ellisland. The Craiks would be in the Riddells' circle of friends, and Burns was probably introduced to Miss Craik at the Riddells' home; obviously they were on friendly terms as she was the author of the lines on the title page of the poetry volume of the Glenriddell MSS.

In this letter Burns treats Miss Craik as a fellow poet, and in doing so, makes some interesting comments on poetry and poets.

59   To John Francis Erskine of Mar (Dumfries, 13th April 1793).

John Francis Erskine of Mar (1741–1825) was the grandson of the Jacobite earl whose titles had been forfeited for his part in the revolution of 1715.

This letter of thanks to Erskine arose from the fact that Burns' outspoken political opinions had resulted in his being denounced to the Board of Excise and that there was an investigation. Burns was badly worried and feared dismissal or at least the ruin of his prospects in the Excise. It says much for the loyalty and power of his friends in high places that the whole matter was smoothed over and that, contrary to general belief, no mention whatever of the incident appeared in Burns' official Excise record. This meant that, so far as promotion was concerned, the incident never happened. This is the only surviving MS. of this letter.

66   To Alexander Cunningham (Dumfries, 10th September 1792).

For note on Alexander Cunningham see Notes p. (32).

Alexander Cunningham married Miss Agnes Moir, youngest daughter of the Rev. Henry Moir, Minister of the Gospel at Auchtertool on 13th April 1792.

73   To Mr. Corbet, Supervisor General of Excise (February ? 1792).

William Corbet (1755–1811). He had a distinguished career in the Excise: his higher posts were Supervisor at Linlithgow (1784), Supervisor General at Stirling (1786–1787), acting Supervisor General at Edinburgh (1789–1791), Supervisor General at Edinburgh (1791–97) and finally collector of Excise at Glasgow (1797). He was one of the people responsible for Burns' success in the Excise. Burns' friend Mrs. Dunlop first brought him to Corbet's attention and continued to use her influence with the Corbets, husband and wife. It was Corbet who probably arranged Burns' transfer to the Dumfries Port Division (see this letter) when the farm of

73   Ellisland was failing. It was Corbet who helped to keep Burns clear of an official reprimand or even dismissal over the 'denunciation' incident. (See letter to Erskine p. 59 of Letters Volume.) In January 1794 Burns says, in a letter to Graham of Fintry, "Mr. Corbet is, I know at the top of the Collector's List, and as they are most of them old men it is extremely probable that the place he holds may be soon vacant. That place—Supervisor-General—is, I understand, nearly secured for Mr. Findlater, my Supervisor here. Could it be possible, then, Sir, that an old Supervisor, who may be still continued, as I know is sometimes the case, after they are rather too infirm for much duty, could not such an Officer be appointed to Dumfries, and so let the officiating job fall to my share? This is a bare possibility, if it be one; so I again beg your pardon for mentioning it." In 1797, when Corbet became Collector for Glasgow, Findlater was, indeed, appointed Supervisor-General in his place, but it was too late to benefit Robert Burns, who had died the previous year.

75   To the Rev. William Moodie, one of the Ministers of Edinburgh (1792).
77   To Alexander Cunningham (11th June 1971).
80   To James Stirling, Provost of Edinburgh—sent by Mr. Clarke, written by Robert Burns (June 1791).
87   To Mr. Williamson, Factor to the Earl of Hopetoun—sent by Mr. Clarke, written by Robert Burns (September 1791).

    These four letters were written by Robert Burns in support of James Clarke (1761–1825), Schoolmaster of Moffat, who was in danger of being dismissed because of alleged severity to some of his pupils. Burns threw himself into this battle largely because he believed a little man was being victimised by powerful people (Lord Hopetoun in particular). Through Burns, Robert Riddell became interested and eventually Clarke was vindicated. Thereafter he had a successful career as schoolmaster, leaving Moffat in 1794 to become master of the Burgh School at Forfar and later becoming rector of the Grammar school at Cupar, Fife. In addition to helping him by writing letters, Burns helped Clarke by lending him money, which Clarke was still repaying at the time of Burns' death.

    This is the only surviving MS. of this letter.

83   To William Smellie, (Dumfries, 22nd January 1792).

    William Smellie (1740–1795) was nineteen years older than Burns. By the time he met Burns he had gained a reputation as printer, publisher, editor and translator but he was not by any means a blameless character. He was the founder of the Crochallan Fencibles and even Burns called him 'Veteran in Genius, wit, and Bawdry.' It was Smellie who printed the 1787 volume, but after Burns left Edinburgh he had little contact with his old printer, though he never forgot him. They kept up a correspon-

83 dence until Smellie's death, but unfortunately the letters which Burns wrote to Smellie between 1788 and 1795 were burned as 'totally unfit for publication'.

Maria Riddell (1771–1808). She was the youngest daughter of William Woodley, Governor and Captain-General of the Leeward Islands. Maria lived in England until she was sixteen, when she went to the West Indies. There, she met Walter Riddell and became his second wife. The couple settled in Woodley Park, near Dumfries, at the end of 1791. They had to leave, however, in 1794, as Walter Riddell could not pay the remainder of the purchase price. The Riddells moved to Tinwald House and later to Halleaths, where they were living at the time of Burns' death. Walter Riddell died in Antigua in 1802: he seems to have wasted his inheritance and to have been a weak character generally. His widow and surviving daughter went south and lived as State pensioners at Hampton Court. In 1807 Maria remarried, but she died the following year. Burns admired Maria greatly and she was undoubtedly the most intellectual of his woman friends. Their friendship had its ups and downs and never seems to have developed into a real love affair, but Maria's *Memoir* written after his death shows how well she understood him.

This letter of introduction to Smellie led to a long friendship between the two and to Smellie printing Maria's book *Voyages to the Madeira and Caribbee Islands*.

85 To Mr. Corbet (Dumfries, September 1792).

This is the only surviving MS. of this letter. It is a letter of thanks to Mr. Corbet for granting the request made in the letter on p. 73 of the Letter volume.

89 To the Duke of Queensberry (Ellisland, 24th September 1791).

William Douglas, fourth Duke of Queensberry (1724–1810). He succeeded his cousin to the dukedom in 1786. Queensberry was Lord of the Bedchamber to George III from 1768–89 but lost favour over the Regency issue and was dismissed from this post. The greatest Landowner in Nithsdale, he was like a king in the locality, but Burns loathed the Duke and wrote some scathing verse about him.

This letter says exactly the opposite of what Burns thought of the Duke, but the note in Burns' hand at the end may offer some explanation; Burns was not averse to being noticed and flattered by the great! The question why Burns should include such a letter in this collection is baffling (For the poem 'the Whistle' sent with this letter see Poetry volume p. 131 and Notes p. (26).)

91   From William Nicol to Robert Burns (10th February 1793).

For a note on William Nicol see Notes p. (31).

This is the famous letter of advice. It was said that Burns refused to rise when God Save the King was played in the Dumfries Theatre; that he joined others in calling for the French Revolutionary song Ca Ira, and that generally he held radical opinions. The matter was investigated and dropped. (See Notes p. (36).)

94   Reply to William Nicol (Dumfries, 20th February 1793).

This is the only surviving MS. source for this letter.

97   To Mrs. Agnes McLehose (Clarinda) (March ? 1793).

For note on Mrs. McLehose see Notes p. (25).

Although the fact is not acknowledged in the Glenriddell text, this is a letter Burns wrote to Clarinda. His note at the end 'I need scarcely remark that the foregoing was the fustian rant of enthusiastic youth' is therefore difficult to explain. The blanks in the Glenriddell MS., taken in order, can be supplied by 'Europe'; 'Peacock'; 'Peacocks'; 'two of my letters, it seems, she never received; and her last, which came when I was in Ayrshire, was unfortunately mislaid, & only found about ten days or a fortnight ago, on removing a desk of drawers'; 'the Scots songs'. This is the only surviving MS. of this letter.

100   To Miss Lessly Bailie of Mayville (Dumfries, May 1793).

Lesley Baillie (d. 1843). She was the daughter of Robert Baillie of Mayville, Ayrshire, and married Robert Cumming of Logie in 1799. She was apparently something of a beauty. Miss Baillie, accompanied by her father and sister, called on Burns in Dumfries in the course of a journey to England. Burns was greatly impressed and wrote *The bonie Lesley Bailie* after their meeting (August 1792). This is the only surviving MS. of this letter. The song enclosed with this letter was *Blythe hae I been on yon hill*.

102   To Miss Davies (August 1791).
Deborah Duff Davies. She was the daughter of Doctor Davies of Tenby, Pembrokeshire. She was in poor health and went abroad to recuperate. Burns wrote several songs to her and the epigram on page 160 of the Poetry volume. Miss Davies died of consumption.

This is the only surviving MS. of this letter.

BIBLIOGRAPHY

In these Notes reference is made to various books by the surname of the author.

FERGUSON: Letters of Robert Burns. Ed. by J. De Lancey Ferguson. 2 v. 1931.

KINSLEY: Poems and Songs of Robert Burns. Ed. by James Kinsley. 3v. 1968.

SNYDER: Life of Robert Burns by Franklyn Bliss Snyder. 1932. Reprinted 1968.

CURRIE: Works of Robert Burns with an account of his life . . . by James Currie. 4v. 1800.

LINDSAY: The Burns encyclopedia, by Maurice Lindsay. 1959. Rev. Ed. 1970.

The Editor acknowledges his indebtedness to the above-named works and to many other sources for information contained in the Notes.

INDEX OF PERSONS REFERRED TO IN THE NOTES

Page numbers of new material in this edition are in parentheses, to distinguish them from those in the facsimile part of the work; the parentheses are, however, omitted from the entries in this Index.

THE
GLENRIDDELL MANUSCRIPTS
OF
ROBERT BURNS

VOLUME I

POEMS

A Description of this volume will be found at page 164.

HAB SHAR

VIRTUS MATURUIT

GLENRIDDELL.

ROBERTUS BURNS SCOTUS.

Poems
(written by)
Mr. Robt. Burns
and
Selected by him from his
unprinted Collection
——— FOR ———
Robert Riddell
of
Glenriddell Esqr.

Here native genius, gay, unique, and strong,
Shines through each page, and marks the tuneful song,
Wrapt Admiration her warm tribute pays,
And Scotia proudly echoes all she says;
Bold Independence too, illumes the theme,
And claims a manly privilege to Fame.
— Vainly, O BURNS! would rank or riches shine,
Compar'd with inborn merit great as thine.
These chance may take, as chance has often giv'n;
But pow'rs like thine, can only come from heav'n.

As this Collection almost wholly consists of pieces local
or unfinished, fragments the effusion of a poetical moment
& bagatelles strung in rhyme simply pour passer le
temps, the Author trusts that nobody into whose hands it
may come will without his permission give or allow to be
taken, copies of any thing here contained; much less
to give to the world at large, what he never meant
should see the light.— At the Gentleman's request, whose
from this time it shall be, the Collection was made;
and to him, & I will add, to his amiable Lady, it is
presented, as a sincere though small tribute of gratitude
for the many many happy hours the Author has
spent under their roof. There, what Poverty
even though accompanied with Genius must seldom
expect to meet with at the tables in the circles
of Fashionable Life, his welcome has ever been,
the cordiality of Kindness, & the warmth of
Friendship. As from the situation in which it
is now placed, this M.S.S. may be preserved, & this
Preface read, when the hand that now writes & the
heart that now dictates it may be mouldering in the
dust; let these be regarded as the genuine sentiments of
a man who seldom flattered any, & never those he loved. —

27th April 179[ ]   ROBt BURNS

Song — Tune – Bonie Dundee —

In Mauchline there dwells six proper young Belles,
    The pride of the place and its neighbourhood a';
Their carriage and dress a stranger would guess,
    In Lon'on or Paris they'd gotten it a':
Miss Miller is fine, Miss Murkland's divine,
    Miss Smith she has wit and Miss Betty is braw;
There's beauty and fortune to get wi' Miss Morton,
    But Armour's [Mrs Burns] the jewel for me o' them a'! —

Note, Miss Armour is now known by the designation
of Mrs Burns —— who has the finest foot & Leg – & had the finest waist
    See. the vision – Coila's leg – compared with bonie Jea's.

Song —   Printed vol 2 p 226

Anna, thy charms my bosom fire,
    And waste my soul with care;
But ah, how bootless to admire,
    When fated to despair!

Yet, in thy presence, lovely Fair,
    To hope may be forgiven;
For sure 'twere impious to despair,
    So much in sight of Heaven!

Epistle to John Goldie in Kilmarnock, Author of, The Gospel recovered —— August — 1785   x $

O Goudie, terror o' the whigs,
Dread o' black coats and reverend wigs!
Sour Bigotry on his last legs
           girns and looks back,
Wishing the ten Egyptian plagues
           May seize you quick.——

Poor gapin, glowrin Superstition!
Waes me, she's in a sad condition:
Fye! bring Black Jock* her state-physician,
               To see her water:
Alas! there's ground for ~~strong~~ great suspicion
           She'll ne'er get better. ——

Enthusiasm's past redemption,
Gane in a gallopin consumption:
Not a' her quacks wi' a' their gumption
           Can ever mend her;
Her feeble pulse gies strong presumption,
           She'll soon surrender.——

Auld Orthodoxy lang did grapple
For every hole to get a stapple,
But now, she fetches at the thrapple
           And fights for breath;

* The Revd. J. R. of U. Kilm. ck

Haste, gie her name up in the Chapel*.
                                    Near unto death. ——

It's you and Taylor‡ are the chief
To blame for a' this black misfhief;
  But could the L—d's ain folk get leave,
                                    A toom tar-barrel

And twa red peats wad bring relief,
                                    And end the quarrel. ——

O For me, my skill's but very sma',
  And skill in Profe I've nane ava;
  But quietlen-wise, between us twa,
                                    Weel may ye speed;
  And tho' they sud you sair misca',
                                    Ne'er fash your head. ——

E'en swinge the dogs; and thresh them sicker,
The mair they squeel ay chap the thicker,
  And still 'mang hands a hearty bicker
                                    O' something stout;
It gars an Owther's pulse beat quicker,
                                    And helps his wit ——

O There's naething like the honeft nappy;
  Whare'll ye e'er see men sae happy,
  Or women sonsie, saft and sappy,
                                    'Tween morn and morn,

*Chapel— Mr. Rufsel's kirk— ‡ Taylor Dr. Taylor of Norwich—

To them wha like to taste the drappie
                    In glass or horn. —

I've seen me daez't upon a time,
I scarce could wink or see a styme;
Just ae hauf-mutchkin does me prime,
                    (Ought less, is little)
Then back I rattle on the rhyme,
                    As gleg's a whittle. —

                    I am &c.

To Miss Jeany Cruikshank, a very young lady, only
child of my much-esteemed friend Mr Cruikshank of
the High-School-Edin.r — Written on the blank
leaf of a book presented to her by the Author —
          Beauteous Rose-bud, young & gay, Printed II 22
          Blooming on the early day;
Never mayst thou, lovely Flower,
Chilly shrink in sleety shower!
Never Boreas' hoary path,
Never Eurus' pois'nous breath,
Never baleful Stellar Lights,
          Taint thee with untimely blights!

Never, never reptile-thief
Riot on thy virgin leaf !!
Nor even Sol too fiercely view
Thy bosom blushing still with dew.'

    Mayst thou long, sweet, crimson Gem,
Richly deck thy native Stem !
Till some evening, sober, calm,
  Dropping dews & breathing 'balm,
  While all around the woodland rings,
  And every bird thy requiem sings,'
Thou amid the dirgeful sound
  Shed thy dying honors round,
  And resign to Parent Earth
The loveliest Form she i'er gave birth. —

Written in 'Friars' Carse' Hermitage. Printed II 160

O Thou whom chance may hither lead,
  Be thou clad in russet weed,
  Be thou deckt in silken stole,
  Grave these maxims on thy soul. ——

        Life is but a DAY at most,
Sprung from night, in darkness lost:
Hope not sunshine every hour;
Fear not clouds will always lour. ——
Happiness is but a name;
Make Content & Ease thy aim:
Ambition is a meteor gleam;
Fame, a restless idle dream:
  Pleasures, insects on the wing
    Round Peace, the tenderest flower of spring
  Those that sip the dew alone,
    Make the butterflies thy own;
  Those that would the bloom devour,
    Crush the locusts, save the Flower. ——

For the Future be prepared;
Guard, wherever thou canst guard:
But thy Utmost duly done,
Welcome what thou canst not shun. —
Follies past, give thou to air;
Make their consequence thy care:
Keep the name of Man in mind,
And dishonor not thy kind. —
Reverence with lowly heart
HIM whose wondrous work thou art;
Keep his Goodness still in view,
Thy trust—and thy example too. —

　　　Stranger, go! Heaven be thy guide!
Quod, the Beadsman of Nid-Side. —

6 On Captn Grose's peregrinations through
Scotland collecting the Antiquities of that kingdom

Hear, Land o' Cakes & brither Scots, Printed I
Frae Maiden-kirk to Johnie Groats!
  If there's a hole in a' your coats,
                              I rede you tent it.
A chield's amang you taking notes,
                              And faith, he'll print it.
If in your bounds ye chance to light
Upon a fine, fat, fodgel wight,
Of stature short, but genius bright,
                              That's he—mark weel—
And wow! he has an unco slight
                              O' cauk & keel. —
By some auld, houlet-haunted biggin,
Or kirk deserted by its riggin,
Its ten to ane ye'll find him snug in
                              Some eldritch part;
Wi' deils, they say, L——d safe's! colleaggin
                              At some black art—

Ilk ghaist that haunts auld ha' or chaumer;
Ye gipsey-gang that deal in glaumor;
And you, deep-read in hell's black grammar,
                    Warlocks & witches,
Ye'll quake at his conjuring hammer,
                    Ye midnight b-tches. —

It's tauld, he was a sodger bred,
And ane wad rather fa'n than fled;
But now he's quat the spurtle-blade,
                    And dog-skin wallet,
And taen the — Antiquarian-trade,
                    I think they call it. —

He has a fouth of auld nick-nackets:
Rousty airn caps, & jinglin jackets
Wad haud the Lowthians three in tackets
                    A towmond gude;
And purvatch-pats, & auld saut-backets,
               : Before the Flood. —
Of Eve's first fire he has a cinder;
Auld Tubalcain's fire-shool & fender;

"O that which distinguished the gender
                              Of Balaam's ass.
A broom-stick of the Witch of Endor,
                              Weel shod wi' brass.—
Forbye, he'll shape you off fu' gleg
The cut of Adam's philibeg;
The knife that nicket Abel's craig,
                              He'll prove you fully,
It twas a faulding jocteleg,
                              Or lang-kail gully. —

But wad ye see him in his glee,
For meikle glee & fun has he;
Then set him down, & twa or three
                              Gude fellows wi' him,
And Port, O Port! shine thou a wee,
                              And then ye'll see him

Now, by the Powers of Verse & Prose,
Thou art a dainty child, O Grose!
Whae'er o' thee shall ill suppose,
                              They sair misca' thee.
I'd take the rascal by the nose
                              Wad say, shame fa' thee!

Ode to the departed Regency-bill – 1789 + $

MS 1   2/8

"1st"
Daughter of Chaos' doting years,
Nurse of ten thousand hopes & fears,
Whether thy airy, unsubstantial Shade
(The rights of sepulture now duly paid)
Spread abroad its hideous form
On the roaring Civil storm,
Deafening din & warring rage
Factions wild with factions wage;
Or underground, deep-sunk, profound,
Among the demons of the earth,
With groans that make the mountains shake,
Thou mourn thy ill-starred, blighted birth;
Or in the uncreated Void,
Where seeds of future-being fight,
With lightened step thou wander wide,
To greet thy Mother – Ancient Night,
And as each jarring, monster mass is past,
Fond recollect what once thou wast:
In manner due, beneath this sacred oak,
Hear, Spirit hear! thy presence I invoke!

By a Monarch's heaven-struck fate!
By a disunited State!
By a generous Prince's wrongs!
By a Senate's strife of tongues!
By a Premier's sullen pride,
Louring on the changing tide!
By dread Thurlow's powers to awe,
Rhetoric, blasphemy & law!
By the turbulent ocean,
A Nation's commotion!
By the harlot-caresses
Of borough-adresses!
By days few & evil!
Thy portion, poor devil!
By power, Wealth, show! the gods by men adored
By Nameless Poverty! their hell abhorred!
By all they hope! By all they fear!
Hear!!! And Appear!!!

Stare not on me, thou ghastly Power;
Nor grim with chained defiance lour:

No Babel-structure would I build
    Where, Order exiled from his native sway,
Confusion may the Regent-sceptre wield,
    While all would rule & none obey:
Go, to the world of Man relate,
    The story of thy sad, eventful fate;
    And call Presumptuous Hope to hear,
    And bid him check his blind career;
    And tell the sore-priest sons of Care,
    Never, never to despair. —

        Paint Charles's speed on wings of fire,
    The object of his fond desire;
    Beyond his boldest hopes, at hand:
    Paint all the triumph of the Portland Band:
    Mark how they lift the joy-exulting voice;
    And how their numerous Creditors rejoice:
But just as hopes to warm enjoyment rise,
Cry, Convalescence! and the vision flies. —

Then next pourtray a darkening twilight gloom
    Eclipsing, sad, a gay, rejoicing morn,

14 While proud Ambition to th' untimely tomb
   By gnashing, grim, despairing fiends is borne:
Paint ruin, in the shape of high D——
   Gaping with giddy terror o'er the brow;
In vain he struggles, the Fates behind him press,
   And clamorous hell yawns for her prey below:
How fallen That, whose pride late scaled the skies!
And This, like Lucifer, no more to rise!
Again pronounce the powerful word;
See Day, triumphant from the night, restored. ——

            Then know this truth, ye Sons of Men!
            (Thus end thy moral tale)
      Your darkest terrors may be vain,
         Your brightest hopes may fail.——

Alteration of the Poem, Page 6.th

Thou whom chance may hither lead,
  Be thou clad in russet weed,
  Be thou deckt in silken stole,
  Grave these counsels on thy soul. —

  Life is but a Day at most,
  Sprung from night, in darkness lost:
  Day, how rapid in its flight!
  Day, how few must see the night!
  Hope not sunshine every hour;
  Fear not clouds will always lour. —

  As Youth & Love with sprightly dance
  Beneath thy morning star advance,
  Pleasure with her siren-air
  May delude the thoughtless pair;
  Let Prudence bless Enjoyment's cup,
  Then, raptured, sip & sip it up. ——

  As thy Day grows warm & high,
  Life's meridian flaming nigh,
  Dost thou spurn the humble vale?
  Life's proud summits wouldst thou scale?

Check thy climbing step, elate,
Evils lurk in felon-wait:
Dangers, eagle-pinioned, bold,
Soar around each cliffy hold;
While chearful Peace with linnet-song
Chants the lowly dells among. ——

As thy shades of evening close,
Beckoning thee to long repose;
As life itself becomes disease,
Seek the chimney-nook of ease. ——
There ruminate with sober thought
On all thou'st seen, & heard, & wrought;
And teach the sportive younker-train,
'Experience' lore, oft bought with pain. ——
Say, Man's true, genuine estimate,
The grand criterion of their fate,
Is not, art thou high, or low?
Did thy fortune ebb, or flow?
Did many talents gild thy span?
Or frugal Nature grudge thee one?

altered:

And teach the sportive younkers round,
Laws of Experience, eagle & sound. —

Tell them, & press it on their mind,
As thou thyself shalt shortly find,
The Smile, or FROWN of aweful Heaven,
To Virtue, or to Vice is given!
Say, to be just, & kind, & wise,
There solid Self-enjoyment lies;
That foolish, selfish, faithless ways,
Lead to be wretched, vile & base. ——

Thus, resigned & quiet, creep
To thy bed of lasting sleep —
Sleep, whence thou shalt ne'er awake,
Night, where dawn shall never break,
Till Future-life, future no more,
To light & joy the Good restore,
To light & joy unknown before. ——

Stranger, go! Heaven be thy guide!
Quod, The Beadsman on Nid-side. ——

Song — Tune, Banks of Banna

1

Yestreen I had a pint o' wine,
  A place where body saw na;
Yestreen lay on this breast o' mine
  The gowden locks of Anna. —
        Israelite
The hungry Jew in wilderness
  Rejoicing o'er his manna,
Was naething to my hiney bliss
  Upon the lips of Anna. _____

2

Ye Monarchs take the East & West,
  Frae Indus to Savannah!
Gie me within my straining grasp
  The melting form of Anna. —
There I'll despise Imperial charms,
  An Empress or Sultana,
While dying raptures in her arms
  I give & take with Anna!!!

For an additional stanza to this song, see page 26.th

Song —

I murder hate by field or flood,
    Tho' glory's name may screen us;
In wars at home I'll spend my blood,
    Life-giving wars of Venus:
The deities that I adore
    Are social Peace & Plenty;
I'm better pleased to <u>make one more</u>,
    Than be the death of twenty. —

I would not die like Socrates,
    For all the fuss of Plato;
Nor would I with Leonidas,
    Nor yet would I with Cato:
The Zealots of the Church, or State,
    Shall ne'er my mortal foes be;
But let me have bold * Zimri's fate,
    Within the arms of Cozbi! —

* Vide. Numbers Chap. 25th Verse 8th — 15th

21. **Holy Willie's Prayer** ‡6‡

Argument — And send the godly in a pet to pray

Pope

Holy Willie was a rather oldish batchelor Elder in the parish of Mauchline, & much & justly famed for that polemical chattering which ends in tippling Orthodoxy, & for that Spiritualized Bawdry which refines to Liquorish Devotion. —— In a Sessional process with a gentleman in Mauchline, a Mr Gavin Hamilton, Holy Willie, & his priest, father Auld, after full hearing in the Presbytry of Ayr, came off but second best; owing partly to the oratorical powers of Mr Robt. Aiken, Mr Hamilton's Counsel; but chiefly to Mr Hamilton's being one of the most irreproachable & truly respectable characters in the country. —— On losing his Process, the Muse overheard him at his devotions, as follows ——

O thou that in the heavens does dwell!
Wha, as it pleases best thysel',
Sends ane to heaven & ten to h—ll
A' for thy glory!
And no for ony gude or ill
They've done before thee. —

I bless & praise thy matchless might,
When thousands thou has left in night,
That I am here before thy sight,
            For gifts & grace,
A burning & a shining light
            To a' this place. —

What was I, or my generation,
That I should get such exaltation?
I, wha deserv'd most just damnation,
            For broken laws'
Sax thousand years ere my creation,
            Thro' Adam's' cause.

When from my mother's womb I fell,
Thou might hae plunged me deep in hell,
To gnash my gooms, & weep, & wail,
            In burning lakes,
Where damned devils roar & yell
            Chain'd to their stakes. —

Yet I am here, a chosen sample,
To shew thy grace is great & ample:
I'm here, a pillar o' thy temple
            Strong as a rock,
A guide, a ruler & example
            To a' thy flock. —

23 But yet—O L—d—confess I must—
At times I'm fash'd wi' fleshly lust;
And sometimes too, in warldly trust
                    Vile Self gets in;
But thou remembers we are dust,
                    Defil'd wi' sin.—

O L—d—yestreen—thou kens—wi' Meg—
Thy pardon I sincerely beg!
O may't ne'er be a living plague,
                    To my dishonor!
And I'll ne'er lift a lawless leg
                    Again upon her.—

Besides, I farther maun avow,
Wi' Leezie's lass, three times—I trow—
But L—d, that friday I was fou
                    When I cam near her;
Or else, thou kens, thy servant true
                    Wad never steer her.—

Maybe thou lets this fleshly thorn
Buffet thy servant e'en & morn,
Lest he o'er proud & high should turn,
                    That he's sae gifted;
If sae, thy hand maun e'en be borne
                    Untill thou lift it.—

L—d bless thy Chosen in this place,
For here thou has a chosen race:
But G—d, confound their stubborn face,
     And blast their name,
Wha bring thy rulers to disgrace
     And open shame. —

L—d mind Gaun Hamilton's deserts!
He drinks, & swears, & plays at cartes,
Yet has sae mony taking arts
     Wi' Great & Sma',
Frae G—d's ain priest the people's hearts
     He steals awa. —

And when we chasten'd him therefore,
Thou kens how he bred sic a splore,
And set the warld in a roar
     O' laughin at us:
Curse thou his basket and his store
     Kail & potatoes. —

L—d hear my earnest cry & prayer
Against that Presbytry of Ayr!
Thy strong right hand, L—d, make it bare
     Upon their heads!
L—d visit them, & dinna spare,
     For their misdeeds!

O L—d my G—d, that glib-tongu'd Aiken!
My very heart & flesh are quaking
To think how I sat, sweating, shaking,
          And pis'd wi' dread,
While Auld wi' hingin lip gaed sneaking
          And hid his head!

L—d, in thy day o' vengeance try him!
L—d visit him that did employ him!
And pass not in thy mercy by them,
          Nor hear their praye
But for thy people's sake destroy them,
          And dinna spare!

But L—d, remember me & mine
Wi' mercies temporal & divine!
That I for grace & gear may shine,
          Excell'd by nane!
And a' the glory shall be thine!
          Amen! Amen!

Epigram —
On Captᵐ F. Grose — Antiquarian — see page 8ᵗʰ

The devil got notice that Grose was a dying,
So, whip! at the summons old Satan came flying;
But when he approach'd where poor Francis lay moaning,
And saw each bed-post with its burden a groaning,
Astonish'd, confounded, cries Satan, by G—!
I'll want him ere take such a damnable load!

Additional stanza to song, page 19ᵗʰ —
Awa, thou flaunting god o'day!
    Awa, thou pale Diana!
Ilk star, gae hide thy twinkling ray!
    When I'm to meet my Anna.
Come, in thy raven plumage, Night;
    Sun, moon & stars withdrawn a';
And bring an angel pen to write
    My transports wi' my Anna. —

Copy of a Letter from Mr. Burns To Doctor Moor

Sir   2 Aug.t 1787
                                   sent 23 Sept.

For some time past I have been rambling over the Country, partly on account of some little business I have to settle in various places; but of late I have been confined with some lingering complaint originating as I take it in the stomach. To divert my spirit a little in this miserable fog of ennui I have taken a whim to give you a history of myself.

My name has made a small noise in the Country. You have done me the honor to interest yourself very warmly in my behalf and I think a faithful account of what character of a man I am and how I came by that character may perhaps amuse you in an idle moment. I will give you an honest narrative though I know it will be at the expence of frequently being laugh'd at. For I assure you, Sir, I have like Solomon whose character, excepting the trifling affair of Wisdom I sometimes think I resemble. I have I say like him turned my eyes to behold madness and folly, and like him too, frequently shaken hands with

their

their intoxicating friendship. In the very
polite letter, Miss Williams did me the honor
to write me she tells me you have got a com
=plaint in your eyes. I pray God it may be
removed; for considering that Lady, and you
are my common friends, you will probably
employ her to read this letter, And then good
night to that esteem with which she was
pleased to honor the Scotch Bard.

After you have perused these pages should
you think them trifling and impertinent—
I only beg leave to tell you, that the poor
Author wrote them under some very
twitching qualms of conscience, that, per-
-haps, he was doing what he ought not to
do: a predicament he has more than once
been in before.

I have not the most distant pretince to what
the stye-coated guardians of Escutcheons
call a Gentleman. When at Edinburgh last
winter I got acquainted at the Heralds Office;
and looking thro' the granary of honors
I there found almost every name in the
Kingdome; but for me

                 cc
—— "My antient but ignoble blood,
    "Has crept thro' Scoundrels since the flood."
Gules, †Purple, Argent &c quite disowned me.
My forefathers rented land of the famous,
noble Keiths of Marshal and had the honor
to share their fate——

† Purpure

I do not use the word honor with any refe=
=rence to political ~~friend or ship~~ principles,
loyal and disloyal I take to be merely relative
terms in that ancient and formidable Court
known in this Country by the name of Club-
=law. Those who dare welcome Ruin and
shake hands with infamy, for what they be-
=leive sincerely to be the cause of their God or
their king, as Mark Anthony in Shakespear
says "Brutus and Cassius are honorable men.
I mention this circumstance because it threw
my father on the world at large, where after
many years wanderings and sojournings,
he picked up a pretty large quantity of obser
=vation and experience to which I am indebted
for most of my little pretensions to Wisdom.
I have met with few who understood Men,
their manners and their ways, equal to him
But stubborn, ungainly Integrity, and head=
=long, ungovernable Irrascibility are disqua=
=lifying circumstances; consequently I was
born a very poor mans son.

For the first six or seven years of my life
my father was Gardener to a worthy gentle=
=man of small Estate in the neighbourhood
of Ayr. Had my father continued in that
situation, I must have marched off to have
been one of the little underlings about a
farm house. but it was his dearest wish
and prayer to have it in his power to keep

his

his children under his own eye till they could
discern between good and evil, so with the af
=sistance of his generous Master he ventured.
on a small farm in that Gentleman's Estate.
At these years I was by no means a favourite
with any body. I was a good deal noted
for a retentive memory, a stubborn, sturdy
something in my disposition, and an enthusi:
=astic idiot piety. I say idiot piety because
I was then but a child. Though I cost the
school-master some thrashings I made an
excellent English Scholar; and against the
years of ten or Eleven I was absolutely a critic
in the substantives verbs and particles. In
my infant and boyish days too, I owed much
to an old maid of my mother's remarkable for
her ignorance, credulity and superstition.
She had I suppose the largest collection in the
Country of tales and songs concerning devils
Ghosts, fairies, browmies, witches, warlockes,
Spunkies, kelpies, ill carvies dead-lights,
wraiths, Apparitions, Cantraips, inchanted
Towers, Giants, dragons and other trumpery
This cultivated the latent seeds of Poesy, but had
so strong an effect on my imagination, that to
this hour, in my nocturnal rambles I sometimes
keep a sharp look out in suspicious places, and
though no body can be more sceptical in these
matters than I, yet it often takes an effort of
Philosophy to shake off these idle Terrors. The

* Elf-candles

earliest thing of composition that I recollect taking pleasure in was the vision of Mirza, and a hymn of Addison's beginning "How are thy Servants blest O Lord" — I particularly remember one half stanza which was music to my boyish ears

"For though in dreadful whirls we hung,
"High on the broken wave"

I met with these pieces in Masons English collection, one of my school-books. The two first books I ever read in private, and which gave me more pleasure than any two books I ever read again, were, the life of Hannibal, and the history of Sir William Wallace. Hannibal gave my young ideas such a turn, that I used to strut in raptures up and down after the recruiting drum and bag-pipe, and wish myself tall enough that I might be a soldier; while the story of Wallace poured a scottish prejudice in my veins, which will boil along there till the flood-gates of life shut in eternal rest. Polemical Divinity about this time was puting the Country half mad; and I ambitious of shining on Sundays between Sermons, in conversation parties at funerals &c, in a few years more used to puzzle Calvinism with so much heat and indiscretion that I raised a hue and cry of heresy against me which has not ceased to this hour.

My vicinity to Ayr was of great advantage to me. My social disposition when not checked by some modification of spited pride, like our Catechism's definition of Infinitude, "was without bounds or limits". I formed many connections with other Younkers, who possessed superior advantages; the youngling Actors, who were busy with the rehearsal of parts in which they were shortly to appear on that stage where Alas! I was destined to drudge behind the scenes. It is not commonly at these green years that the young Noblesse and Gentry have a just sense of the immense distance between them and their ragged play-fellows. It takes a few dashes into the world to give the young great Man that proper, decent, unnoticing disregard for the poor, insignificant, stupid devils, the Mechanics and peasantry around him who perhaps were born in the same Vil-lage. — My young superiours never insulted the clouterly appearance of my ploughboy carcase, the two extremes of which were often ex-posed to all the inclemency of all the seasons. They would give me stray volumes of books; Among them even then I could pick up some observations; And one whose heart I am sure not even the Munny Begum's scenes have tainted, helped me to a little French. Parting

with

with these, my young friends and benefactors
as they dropped off for east or west Indies, was
often to me a sore affliction. But I was soon
called to more serious evils. My fathers gene
=rous Master died; the farm proved a ruinous
bargain, and to clench the curse we fell into
the hands of a Factor who sat for the picture
I have drawn of one in my tale of "twa dogs".
My father was advanced in life when he married.
I was the eldest of seven children And he worn
out by early hardship, was unfit for labor. My
fathers spirit was soon irritated, but not easily
broken. There was a freedom in his lease in two
years more, and to weather these, we retrenched
~~in~~ expences. +He lived very poorly. I was a
dextrous Plough-man for my years, and the
next eldest to me was a Brother who could drive
the plough very well, and help me to thrash.
A novel-writer might perhaps have viewed
these scenes with some satisfaction; but so did
not I. My indignation yet boils at the threat:
=ening, insolent Epistles from the Scoundrel
Tyrant which used to set us all in tears.
   This kind of life the chearless gloom of a
hermit with the unceasing toil of a Galley-slave
brought me to my sixteenth year, & little before
which period I first committed the sin of Rhyme.
You know our Country custom of coupling a
man and woman together as partners in the

labors

+He

Labors of Harvest. In my fifteenth autumn.
my partner was a bewitching creature who just
counted an autumn less. My scarcity of
English denies me the power of doing her
justice in that language, but you know the
scotch idiom She was a bonie sweet, sonsy lass. —
In short she, altogether unwittingly to herself
initiated me into a certain delicious passion,
which, in spite of acid disappointment, gin-
horse prudence, and book-worm Philosophy
I hold to be the first of human joys, our chiefest
pleasure here below. How she caught the contagion
I can't say, you medical folks talk much of
infection by breathing the same air, the touch &c
but I never expressly told her that I loved her In-
-deed I did not well know myself, why I liked so
much to loiter behind with her, when returning
in the evening from our labors; why the tones
of her voice made my heart-strings thrill like
an Eolian harp, and particularly why my pulse
beat such a furious Rantann, when I looked
and fingered over her hand to pick out the nettle
stings and thistles. Among her other love-inspir-
-ing qualifications, she sung sweetly, and 'twas
her favourite scotch Reel that I attempted to give
an embodied vehicle to in rhyme. I was not so
presumptive as to imagine that I could make
verses like printed ones, composed by men who
had Greek and Latine but my Girl sung a song.
which was said to be composed by a small

country

Country Laird's son, on one of his father's maids with whom he was in love. And I saw no reason why I might not rhyme as well as he; for excepting smearing sheep, and casting peats, his father living in the moors, he had no more scholar-craft than I had.

Thus with me began love and poesy, which at times have been my only, and till within this last twelvemonth have been my highest enjoyment.

My father struggled on till he reached ~~the~~ a freedom in his lease, when he entered on a larger farm, about ten miles farther in the country. The nature of the bargain was such as to throw a little ready money in his hand at the commence=ment, otherwise the affair would have been un=practicable. For four years we lived comfortably here, but a law-suit between him and his land-lord commencing, after three years tossing and whirling in the vortex of Litigation, my father . was just saved from absorption in a jail by a phthisical consumption, which after two years pro=mise, kindly stept in and snatched him away to where the wicked cease from troubling, and where the weary are at rest.

It is during this climacterick that my little story is most eventful. I was at the beginning of this period, perhaps the most ungainly, awkward being in the parish. No Solitaire was less acquain=ted with the ways of the world. My knowledge of ancient story was gathered from Guthrie's and Salmon's Geographical Grammar. My knowledge of modern manners, and of literature and criticism I got from the Spectator. These with Pope's

works

works; some plays of Shakespear, Tull, and Dickson on agriculture, the Pantheon, Locke's Essay on the human understanding, Stackhouse's history of the Bible, Justice's British Gardener, Boyle's lectures, Allan Ramsay's works, Doctor Taylor's scripture doctrine of original sin, a select collection of English songs, and Hervey's meditations had been the extent of my reading. The collection of songs was my vade-mecum. I pored over them driving my cart, or walking to labor song by song, verse by verse, carefully noting the tender or sublime from affectation and fustain. I am convinced I owe much to this for my critick-craft such as it is.

In my seventeenth year to give my manners a brush, I went to a country dancing school. My father had an unaccountable antipathy against these meetings, and my going was what to this hour I repent in absolute defiance of his commands. My father as I said before was the sport of strong passions; from that instance of rebellion he took a kind of dislike to me; which I believe was one cause of that dissipation which marked my future years. I only say dissipation comparative with the strictness and sobriety of Presbyterian country life; for though the Will-o'-wisp, meteors of thoughtless whim were almost the sole lights of my path, yet early ingrained piety and virtue never failed to point me out the line of innocence. The great misfortune of my life was never to have an aim. I had felt early some stirrings of ambition, but they were the blind gropings of Homer's Cyclops round the

walls

walls of his cave. I saw my father's situation
entailed on me perpetual labour. The only two
doors by which I could enter the fields of fortune
were, the most niggardly Œconomy, or the little
chicaning art of bargain-making. The first is so
contracted an aperture, I never could squeeze my
self into it, the last I always hated the contamina =
=tion of the threshold. Thus abandoned of view
or aim in life with a strong appetite for sociability
as well from native hilarity as from a pride of
observation and remark. a constitutional hypo=
=condriac taint which made me fly solitude, Add
to all these incentives to social life, my reputation for
bookish knowledge, a certain wild logical talent, and
a strength of thought, something like the rudiments of
good sense made me generally a welcome guest
So 'tis no great wonder that always "where two or three
"were met together, there was I in the midst of them"
But far beyond all the other impulses of my
heart, was un penchant à l'adorable moitié
du genre humain. My heart was completely
tinder, and was eternally lighted up by some
Goddess or other: And like every warfare in this
world, I was sometimes crowned with success,
and sometimes mortified with defeat. At the
plough, scythe or reap-hook I feared no com=
=petitor, and set want at defiance; And as I
never cared farther for any labor than while
I was in actual exercise, I spent the evening in
the way after my own heart. A country lad
rarely carries on an Amour without an af=

sisting

assisting confident. I possessed a curiosity,
zeal, and intrepid dexterity in these matters
which recommended me as a proper second in
duels of that kind, and I dare say, I felt as
much pleasure at being in the secret of half
the amours in the parish, as ever did Premier
at knowing the intrigues of half the courts of
Europe.

The very goose-feather in my hand seems in-
stinctively to know the well worn path of my
imagination, the favourite theme of my song,
and is with difficulty restrained from giving
you a couple of paragraphs on the amours of my
compeers, the humble inmates of the farm-house,
and cottage; but the grave sons of science, ambition
or avarice, baptize these things by the name of
follies. To the sons and daughters of labour and
poverty, they are matters of the most serious
nature. To them the ardent hope—the stolen in-
terview—the tender farewell, are the greatest,
and most delicious part of their enjoyments.

Another circumstance in my life which
made very considerable alterations on my mind
and manners was, I spent my seventeenth summer a good distance from home, at a noted
school, on a smuggling coast, to learn mensura-
tion, surveying, dialling &c; in which I made
a pretty good progress.—But I made greater progress in the knowledge of mankind. The contra-
=band trade was at this time very successful,

scenes

Scenes of swaggering, riot and roaring dissipation
were as yet new to me, and I was no enemy to
social life. Here, though I learned to look uncon-
cernedly on a large Tavern-bill, an amix without
fear in a drunken squable, yet I went on with a
high hand in my geometry, till the sun entered
Virgo, a month which is always a carnival in
my bosom, a charming Fillette who lived next
door to the school, overset my Trigonometry, and
set me off in a Tangent from the sphere of my
studies. I struggled on with my ~~tinny~~ and + sines

*† co-sines *~~and~~ for a ~~few~~ days more, but ~~~~ out to
the Garden one charming noon to take the
Suns altitude I met with my Angel!

⟨"⟩
— Like Proserpine gathering flowers
⟨"⟩ Herself a fairer flower —

It was vain to think of doing any more good
at school. The remaining week I staid I did
nothing but craze the faculties of my soul about
her, or steal out to meet with her. And the two
last nights of my stay in the Country, had sleep
been a mortal sin, I was innocent.

I returned home very considerably improved.
My reading was enlarged with the very important addition of Thomson's and Shenston's
works. I had seen mankind in a new phasis,
and I engaged several of my school-fellows to
keep up a literary correspondence with me.
This last helped me on much in composition.
I had met with a collection of letters, by the
Wits of Queen Ann's reign, and I pored over
them

them most devoutly. I kept copies of any of
my own letters that pleased me, and a comparison
between them and the composition of most of
my correspondents, flattered my vainity. I
carried this whim so far, that though I had not
three farthings worth of bussiness in the world
yet every post brought me as many letters as
if I had been a broad plodding son, of day-
=book and ledger.

My life flowed on, much in the same tenor
till my twenty-third year, Vive l'amour
et Vive la bagatelle were my sole principles
of action. The addition of two more authors to
my library gave me great pleasure. Sterne
and M'Kinzie—Tristram shandy and the
man of Feeling were my bosom favourites.
Poesy was still a darling walk for my mind,
I had usually half a dozen or more pieces on
hand. I took up one or other, but it was only
the humour of the hour. I had usually half
a dozen or more pieces on hand. I took up one
or other as it suited the momentary tone of
the mind, and dismissed it as it bordered
on fatigue. My passions when once they
were lighted up, raged like so many devels
till they got vent in Rhyme, and then conning
over my verses, like a spell, soothed all into quiet.
None of the Rhymes of those days are in print,
except Winter a dirge, the eldest of my printed
pieces, the death and dying words of poor
                                        Maulie

Mauchline, John Barleycorn, and Songs first, and second, and third. Song second was the ebullition of that passion which ended the foremention'd school-business .

My twenty third year was to me an important era, partly through whim, and partly that I wished to set about doing something in life. I joined with a flax-dresser in a neighbouring Country Town, to learn his trade, and carry on the business of manufactoring and retailing flax. This turned out a sadly, unlucky affair, My partner was a scoundrel of the first water, who made money by the mystery of Theiving, and to finish the whole, while we were giving a welcoming carousal to the new year, our shop burnt to ashes, and left me, like a true Poet, not worth six pence. I was obliged to give up business, the clouds of misfortune were gathering thick round my Father's head, the darkest of which was, he was visibly far gone in a consumption. The finishing evil that brought up the rear of this infernal file was my hypocondriac complaint being irritated to such a degree that for three months I was in a diseased state of body, and mind, scarcely to be envied by the hopeless wretches who have just got their sentence, "Depart from me ye cursed &c .

From this adventure I learned something of a Town life; but the principal thing which gave my mind a turn was, I formed a

bosom

No town all a belle fille whom I adored gone and who had pledged her soul to meet me in the fields of matrimony jilted me with peculiar circumstances of mortification.

bosom friendship with a young fellow, the
first created being, I had ever seen, but a hap:
:less son of misfortune. He was the son of a
plain Mechanic, but a great man in the neigh:
:bourhood, taking him under his patronage,
gave him a Genteel Education, with a veiw
to bettering his situation in life. The Patron
dying, and leaving my friend unprovided
for, just as he was ready to launch forth into
the world, the poor fellow in dispair, went
to sea; where after a variety of good and
bad fortune, he was a little before I was ac:
:quainted with him, set ashore by an
American Privateer, on the wild coast of
Connaught, striptt of everything. I cannot
quit this poor fellow's story, without adding,
that he is at this moment, Captain of a large
Westindiadman, belonging to the Thames.

        This Gentleman's mind, was fraught with
courage, independance and magnanimity,
and every noble manly virtue. I loved him,
I admired him to a degree of enthusiasm,
and I strove to imitate him. I in some measure
succeeded. I had the pride before, but he
taught it to flow, in proper channels. His
Knowledge of the world, was vastly superior
to mine; and I was all attention to learn. He
was the only man I ever saw, who was a
greater fool than myself, when Woman was

                                        the

presiding

the ~~prevailing~~ star, but he spoke of a certain fashionable feeling with levity, which hitherto I had regarded with horror. Here his friendship did me a mischief and the consequence was, that soon after I resumed the plough, I wrote the welcome, inclosed.

My reading was only encreased by two stray volumes of Pamela, and one of Ferdinand Count Fathom, which gave me some idea of Novels. Rhyme, except some religious pieces, which are in print, I had given up; but meeting with Ferguson's Scotch Poems, I strung anew my wildly-sounding, rustic lyre, with emulating vigor. When my Father died, his all went among the rapacious hell-hounds, that grovel in the kennel of justice. but we made a shift to scrape a little money, in the family amongst us; with which, to keep us together, my Brother and I took a neighbouring farm. My Brother wanted my hare-brained imagination, as well as my social and amorous madness; but in good sense, and every sober qualification, he was far my superior.

I entered on this farm with a full resolution "come," "go to, I will be wise". I read farming books, I calculated crops. I attended markets, and in short, in spite of the devil, the world, and the flesh; I beleive I should have been a wise man; but the first year, from

un=

unfortunately buying in bad seed. The se=
=cond, from a late harvest, we lost half of both
our crops. This overset all my wisdom, and I
returned like the dog to his vomit, and the
sow that was washed, to her wallowing in
the mire. I now began to be known in the
neighbourhood as a maker of Rhymes. The
first of my poetic offspring that saw the light,
was a burlesque lamentation on a quarrel
between two Reverend Calvinists, both Dramatis
personae in my holy Fair. I had an idea
myself, that the piece had some merit: but
to prevent the worst, I gave a copy of it to a friend
who was very fond of these things, and told him
I could not guess who was the author of it, but that
I thought it pretty clever. With a certain side
of both Clergy and Laity it met with a roar of ap
=plause— Holy Willie's Prayer next made its
appearance, and alarmed the Kirk Session so
much, that they held three several meetings to
look over their holy artillery if any of it was
pointed against profane Rhymes. Unluckily
for me my idle wanderings led me on another
side, point blank, within reach of their heaviest
metal this is the unfortunate story alluded to
in my printed poem, the Lament. 'Twas a shoc=
=king affair, which I cannot yet bear to recollect,
and very nearly given me one or two of the
principal qualifications for a place amongst
those who have lost the chart, and mistake the

reckoning

reckoning of nationality. I gave up my part
of the farm to my Brother, as in truth it was
only nominally mine; for Stock I had none to
embark in it, and made what little preparation
was in my power for Jamaica. Before leaving
my native country, however, I resolved to pub=
=lish my poems. I weighed my productions as
impartially as in my power; I thought they had
merit, and it was a delicious idea that I should
be called a clever fellow, even tho' it should never
reach my ears, a poor Negro driver, or perhaps
gone to the world of spirits, a victim to that inhos=
=pitable clime. I can truly say that ~~for ever i~~ paun'd
~~me~~ as I then was, I had pretty nearly as high an
idea of myself, and my works, as I have this mo=
=ment. ~~It was ever my opinion,~~ that the great un=
=happy mistakes, and blunders, both in a national
and religious point of view, of which we see thous=
=ands daily guilty, are owing to their ignorance
or mistaken notions of themselves. To know my=
=self, had been all along my constant study. I
weighed myself alone. I ballanced myself with
~~others~~. I watched every means of information
how much ground I occupied as a man and
as a poet. I studied asidiously nature's design;
where she seemed to have intended the various
lights and shades in my character. I was pretty
sure my poems would meet with some applause
but at the worst, the roar of the Atlantic
                                        would.

incomming

would deafen the voice of censure, and the no
velty of West Indian scenes would make me
forget Neglect. I threw off six hundred Copies
of which, I had got subscriptions for about three hundred
and fifty. My vanity was highly gratified by
the reception I met with from the public, besides
pocketing, all expences deducted, near twenty
pounds. This last came very seasonably, as I
was about to indent myself for want of money
to pay my freight. So soon as I was master of nine
guineas, the price of wafting me to the Torrid Zone
I bespoke a passage in the very first ship that was
to sail; for

"Hungry Ruin had me in the wind"—

I had for some time been skulking from covert
to covert, under all the terrors of a jail; as some
ill advised ungrateful people had uncoupled
the merciless legal pack at my heels. I had ta:
-ken the last farewell of my few friends. My
chest was on the road to Greenock. I had com:
-posed the Song "The gloomy night is gathering
fast", which was to be the last effort of my Muse
in Caledonia, when a letter from Dr Blacklock
to a friend of mine overthrew all my schemes
by rousing my poetic ambition. The Doctor be
-longed to a class of critics, for whose applause I
had not even dared to hope—His idea that I
would meet with every encouragement for a
second Edition fired me so much, that away
I posted for Edinburgh without a single acquain:
-tance in Town, or a single letter of recommendation
in my pocket. The baneful Star that had so long
presided in my Zenith, for once made a revo

lution

see Dalziels
Letter

revolution to the Nadir; and the providential care
of a good God placed me under the Patronage of
one of his noblest creatures, the Earl of Glencairn
" Oubliez moi, grand dieu si jamais je l'oublié. —

I need relate no farther— At Edinburgh
I was in a new world: I mingled among many
classes of men, but all of them new to me, and
I was all attention "to catch the manners, living
"as they rise".

You can now Sir, form a pretty near guess of
what sort of a Wight he is, whom for sometime
you have honored with your correspondence—
That Whim and Fancy, keen sensibility and
riotous passions may still make him zig, zag
in his future path of life is very probable; but
come what will, I shall answer for him the most
determinate integrity and honor, and though
his evil star should again blaze in his meri=
=dian, with tenfold more direful influence, he
may relucktanly tax friendship with Pity
but no more

My most respectful Complements to Miss Williams
very Elegant and friendly letter she honored
me with a few days ago, I cannot answer at pre
=sent, as my presence is requisite at Edinburgh
for a week or so, and I set off tomorrow

I enclose you Holy Willie's for the sake of giving
you a little farther information of the affair than
Mr Creech could do— An Elegy I composed the
other day on Sir James H. Blair, if time
          allow

allow I will transcribe. Its merit is just
mediocre

     With the most grateful respect I have the honor to be

Sir,

       Your very humble Servant ——

(signed)   Robert Burns

Mauchline 2 August 1707½ .

       Direct to me at Mauchline Ayrshire ——

Know all whom it may concern, that I, the Author, am not
answerable for the false spelling & injudicious punctuation in
the foregoing transcript of my letter to Dr Moore. —— I have
something generous in my temper that cannot bear to see
or hear the Absent wronged. & I am very much hurt to
that in several instances the transcriber has injured & many
mangled the proper name & principal title of a Personage
of the very first distinction in all that is valuable among
men, Antiquity, abilities & power; (Virtue, every body knows is
an obsolete business) I mean, the Devil. —— Considering
that the Transcriber was one of the Clergy, an order that owe
the very bread they eat to the said Personage's exertions, the
affair was absolutely unpardonable. —— R. B. ——

(49)

When Captain Grose was at Friars-Carse,
in Summer 1790. Collecting materials for his
Scottish Antiquities he applied to Mr. Burns then
living in the neighbourhood to write him an
account of the Witches meetings at Alloway Church,
near Ayr who complied with his request and wrote
for him the following Poem.

Tam o' Shanter
A Tale   Printed 11   195

When chapmen billies leave the street,
And drouthy neebors, neebors meet,
As market-days are wearing late,
And folk begin to tak the Gate;
While we sit bowsing at the nappy,
And getting fou, and unco happy,
We think na on the lang Scots miles,
The waters, mosses, slaps and Styles,
That lie between us and our hame;
Where sits our Sulky, Sullen dame,
Gathering her brows, like gathering Storm
Nursing her wrath to keep it warm.

This truth fand honest Tam o' Shanter,
As he frae Ayr ae night did canter;
(Auld Ayr, whom ne'er a Town surpasses
For honest men and bonnie lasses)

O Tam! hadst thou but been sae wise,
As taen thy ain wife Kate's advice!
She tauld thee weel, thow was a Skellum,
A blethrin, blusterin, drunken blellum;
That frae November till October,
Ae market-day thow was na sober;
That ilka melder, wi' the Miller,
Thow sat as lang as thow had siller;
That every naig was ca'd a shoe on,
The Smith and thee gat roaring fou on;
That at the L—d's house even on Sunday,
Thow drank wi' Kirkton Jean till monday;
She prophesied that, late or soon,
Thow wad be found deep-drown'd in Doon;
Or catch'd wi' warlocks in the mirk,
By Alloway's auld haunted Kirk. —

Ah, gentle Dames! it gars me greet,
To think how mony counsels sweet,
How mony lengthen'd, sage advices,
The Husband frae the wife despises!

But to our tale —— ae market night,
Tam had got planted unco right,
Fast by an ingle bleezing finely,
Wi' reaming Swats that drank divinely,
And at his elbow Souter Johnie,
His ancient, trusty, drouthy cronie;
Tam lo'ed him like a vera brither,
They had been fou for weeks thegither.
The night drave on wi' sangs and clatter,
And ay the ale was growing better,
The Landlady and Tam grew gracious,
Wi' favors, secret, sweet and precious,
The Souter tauld his queerest stories,
The Landlord's laugh was ready chorus;
The Storm without might rair and rustle,
Tam did na mind the Storm a whistle.
Care mad to see a man sae happy
E'en drown'd himsel amang the nappy:

As bees flee hame wi' lades o' treasure,
The minutes wing'd their way wi' pleasure:
Kings may be blest, but Tam was glorious,
O'er a' the ills o' life victorious!

But pleasures are like poppies spread,
You sieze the flower, its bloom is shed;
Or like the snow falls in the river,
A moment white — then melts for ever;
Or like the Borealis race,
That flit ere you can point their place;
Or like the rainbow's lovely form,
Evanishing amid the storm. —
Nae man can tether, Time, or Tide;
The hour approaches Tam maun ride;
That hour o' night's black arch the key-stane
That dreary hour he mounts his Beast in;
And sic a night he taks the road in
As ne'er poor Sinner was abroad in.

The wind blew, as 'twad blawn its last;
The rattling showers rose on the blast;
The speedy gleams the darkness swallow'd.
Loud, deep, and lang, the thunder bellow'd:

That night a child might understand:
The Deil had business on his hand.

Weel mounted on his grey Meare, Meg,
A better never lifted leg,
Tam skelpit on thro' dub and mire,
Despising wind, and rain and fire.
Whyles holding fast his gude blew bonnet;
Whyles crooning o'er an auld Scots sonnet;
Whyles glowring round w' prudent cares,
Lest bogles catch him unawares:
Kirk-Aloway was drawing nigh,—
Where ghaists and houlets nightly cry.

By this time he was cross the ford,
Where in the snaw the chapman smoor'd,
And past the birks and meikle stane,
Where drunken Charlie brak's neck-bane;
And thro' the whins and by the cairn
Where hunters fand the murder'd bairn;
And near the thorn, aboon the well,
Where Mungo's Mither hang'd hersel.
Before him, Doon pours all his floods;
The doubling storm roars thro' the woods;

The lightenings flash from pole to pole;
Near, and more near the Thunders roll;
When, glimmering thro' the groaning trees,
Kirk-Aloway seem'd in a bleeze
Thro' ilka bore the beams were glancing,
And loud resounded Mirth and Dancing.

Inspiring, bold John Barleycorn!
What dangers thou canst make us scorn:
Wi' Tippeny, we fear nae evil;
Wi' Usquabae we'll face the Devil!
The swats sae ream'd in Tammie's noddle,
Fair play, he car'd na deils a boddle,
But Maggie stood, right sair astonish'd,
Till by the heel and hand admonish'd,
She ventur'd forward on the light;
And, Wow! Tam saw an unco sight!

Warlocks and Witches in a dance,
Nae cotillon brent new frae France
But hornpipes, jigs, Strathspeys and reels,
Put life and mettle in their heels.
A winnock-bunker in the east,
Where sat auld Nick in shape o' beast--

A tousie tyke black, grim and large

To gie them Music was his charge

He screw'd the pipes and gart them skirl,

Till roof and rafters a' did dirl.

Coffins stood round, like open Presses

That shaw'd the dead in their last dresses

And (by some devilish cantraip slight,)

Each in its cauld hand held a light.

By which heroic Tam was able,

To note upon the haly table,

A murderers banes, in gibbet airns,

Twa span-lang, wee, unchristen'd bairns;

A Thief new cutted frae a rape,

Wi' his last gasp his gab did gape

Five Tomahawks, wi' blood red-rusted;

Five Scymitars, wi' murder crusted;

A garter which a babe had strangled;

A knife a father's throat had mangled;

Whom his ain son of life bereft,

The grey hairs yet stak to the heft:

Wi' mair of horrible and awfu',

That even to name wad be unlawfu'

Three Lawyers tongues turn'd inside out,

Wi' lies seem'd like a beggars clout;

Three Priests hearts, rotten black as muck
Say stinking vile in every neuk.

As Tammie glow'd, amaz'd and curious,
The mirth and fun grew fast and furious:
The Piper loud and louder blew;
The Dancers quick and quicker flew;
They reel'd, they set, they cross'd they cleek it
Till ilka Carlin swat and reekit,
And coost her duddies on the work
And linked at it in her Sark.

Now Tam! O Tam! had thae been Queans
N' plump and strappin in thur teens!
Thur Sarks instead o' creeshie flainen,
Been snaw-white, seventeen hunder linen
Thir breeks o' mine, my only pair,
That ance were plush o' gude blue hair
I wad hae gien them off my hurdies,
For ae blink o' the bonie burdies!
But withered beldames, auld and droll,
Rigwoodie hags wad spean a foal,
Loupin and flingin on a crummock,
I wonder did na turn thy stomach.

But Tam ken'd what was what fu' brawlie
There was ae winsome wench and walie

That night enlisted in the core,
(Lang after kend on Carrick shore,
For mony a beast to dead she shot,
And piers'd mony a bonnie boat,
And shook baith meikle corn and bear,
And kept the country-side in fear.)
Her cutty-sark o' Paisley harn,
That while a lassie she had worn,
In longitude tho' sorely scanty,
It was her best, and she was vauntie.
Ah! little thought thy reverend grannie
That sark she coft for her wee Nannie,
Wi' twa pund Scots ('twas a her riches)
Should ever grac'd a dance o' witches!

            But here my Muse her wing maun cour,
Sic flights are far beyond her power,
To sing how Nannie lap and flang
(A souple jad she was and strang,)
And how Tam stood like ane bewitch'd,
And thought his very een enrich'd;
Even Satan glowr'd, and fidg'd fu' fain,
And hotch'd and blew wi' might and main;

Till first ae caper — syne anither

Tam lost his reason a' thegither

And roars out—"Weel done cutty sark!"

And in an instant all was dark;

And scarcely had he maggie rallied,

When out the hellish legion sallied.

As bees bizz out wi' angry fyke,

When plundering herds assail their byke;

As open Pussie's mortal foes;

When pop she starts before their nose;

As eager rins the market croud,

When "catch the Thief!" resounds aloud;

So Maggie rins, the Witches follow,

Wi' mony an eldritch shout and hollois

Ah! Tam! Ah! Tam! thou'll get thy fairin!

In hell they'll roast thee like a herrin!

In vain thy Kate awaits thy comin,

Kate soon will be a woefu' woman.

Now, do thy speedy utmost, Meg!

And win the key-stane o' the brig!

There at them thou thy tail may toss

A running Stream they dare na cross!

But ere the key-stane she could make,
The fient a tail she had to shake.
For Nannie far before the rest,
Hard upon noble Maggie prest,
And flew at Tam wi' furious ettle;
But little wist she Maggie's mettle,
Ae spring brought off her master hale,
But left behind her ain grey tail:
The Carlin claught her by the rump,
And left poor Maggie scarce a stump.

Now wha this Tale o' truth shall read,
Ilk man and Mither's Son, tak heed:
Whene'er to Drink you are inclin'd,
Or Cutty-Sarks rin in your mind,
Think, ye may buy the joys o'er dear,
Remember Tam o' Shanter's Meare.

On the death of Sir James Hunter Blair —

The lamp of day with ill-presaging glare,
   Dim, cloudy, sunk beneath the western wave:
Th' inconstant blast howl'd thro' the darkening air
   And hollow whistled in the rocky cave. —

Lone as I wander'd by each cliff and dell,
   * And the lov'd haunts of Scotia's royal train;
Or mus'd where limpid streams, once hallow'd well,*
   Or mouldring ruins mark the sacred Fane.* —

Th' increasing blast roar'd round the beetling rocks,
   The clouds swift-wing'd flew o'er the starry sky,
The groaning trees untimely shed their locks,
   And shooting Meteors caught the startled eye. —

The paly Moon rose in the livid east,
   And 'mong the cliffs disclos'd a stately Form,
In weeds of woe, that frantic beat her breast,
   And mix'd her wailings with the raving storm. —

---

  * The King's park at Holyrood house. —
  * St Anthony's well. —
  * St Anthony's Chapel. —   Wild

Wild to my heart the filial pulses glow,
 'Twas Caledonia's trophy'd shield I view'd:
Her form majestic droop'd in pensive woe,
 The lightening of her eye in tears embued. —

Reverse'd that spear redoubtable in war,
 Reclin'd that banner, erst in fields unfurl'd,
That like a deathful meteor gleam'd afar —
 And brav'd the mighty Monarchs of the world! —

"My patriot son fills an untimely grave!"
 With accents wild I lifted arms she cry'd;
"Low lies the hand that oft was stretch'd to save,
 Low lies the heart that swell'd w.t honor's pride!

A weeping Country joins a Widow's tear,
 The helpless Poor mix with the Orphan's cry;
The drooping Arts surround their Patron's bier,
 And grateful Science heaves the heart felt sigh.

I saw my sons resume their ancient fire;
 I saw fair Freedom's blossoms richly blow:
But ah, how Hope is born but to expire!
 Relentless Fate has laid their Guardian low. —

My

My patriot falls, but shall he lie unsung
 While empty Greatness saves a worthless name?
No; every Muse shall join her tuneful tongue,
 And future ages hear his growing fame. —
O And I will join a Mother's tender cares,
 Thro' future times to make his virtues last,
That distant years may boast of other Blairs" —
 She said, & vanish'd with the sweeping blast. —

The Performance is but mediocre, but my grief was sincere. —
The last time I saw the worthy, public spirited man — A Man
he was! How few of the two-legged breed that pass for such,
deserve the designation? — he pressed my hand, & asked
me with the most friendly warmth if it was in his
power to serve me; & if so, that I would obledge him
by telling him how. — I had nothing to ask of him,
but if ever a child of his should be so unfortunate as
to be under the necessity of asking any thing of
so poor a man as I am, it may not be in my
power to grant it, but, by G— I shall try!!!

Written on the blank leaf of a copy of the first
Edition of my Poems which I presented to an Old
Sweet-Heart, then married ————

Once fondly lov'd, & still remember'd dear,
    Sweet early Object of my youthful vows,
Accept this mark of Friendship, warm, sincere,
    Friendship! 'tis all cold Duty now allows. —

And when You read the simple, artless ryhmes,
    One friendly sigh for him, he asks no more,
Who distant burns in flaming torrid climes,
    Or haply lies beneath th' Atlantic roar. —

'Twas the girl I mention in my letter to Dr Moore,
where I speak of taking the sun's altitude. ——
Poor Peggy! Her husband is my old acquaintance & a most
worthy fellow. — When I was taking leave of my Carrick
relations intending to go to the West Indies, when I took farewel of
her, neither she nor I could speak a syllable. — Her husband

On reading in a Newspaper the death of J. Mc
-Leod Esquire, brother to Miss Isabella McLeod a par-
-ticular friend of the Author. ―――

Printed || 227

Sad thy tale thou idle page,
    And rueful thy alarms;
Death tears the brother of her love
    From Isabella's arms. ―――

Sweetly deckt with pearly dew
    The morning rose may blow,
But cold, successive noontide blasts
    May lay its beauties low.

Fair on Isabella's morn
    The sun propitious smil'd,
But long ere noon, succeeding clouds
    Succeeding hopes beguil'd. ―――

Tale
ed me three miles on my road, & we both parted with
tears.

Fate oft tears the bosom chords
    That Nature finest strung:
So Isabella's heart was form'd
    And so her heart was wrung. —

Dread Omnipotence alone
    Can heal the wound he gave,
Can point the grief-worn ~~eyes~~ brimful eyes
    To scenes beyond the grave. —

Virtue's blossoms there shall blow,
    And fear no withering blast:
There Isabella's spotless worth
    Shall happy be at last. —

This poetic compliment, what few poetic compliments a
was from the heart. —

Epitaph on a Friend

An honest man here lies at rest,
As e'er God with his image blest.
The friend of man, the friend of truth;
The friend of Age, & guide of Youth:
Few hearts like his with Virtue warm'd
Few heads with Knowledge so inform'd:
If there's another world, he lives in bliss;
If there is none, he made the best of this.

Printed 11 22

The humble petition of Bruar Water to
the Noble Duke of Athole. ——

—— O Bruar falls are the finest in the Country,
but not a bush about them which spoils
much their beauty ——

My Lord, I know your noble ear
    Woe ne'er assails in vain;
Embolden'd thus I beg you'll hear
    Your humble slave complain,
How saucy Phebus' scorching beams,
    In flaming summer-pride,
Dry-withering, waste my foamy streams,
    And drink my crystal tide. ——

The lightly-jumping, glowing trouts
    That thro' my waters play,
When in their random, wanton spouts
    They near the margin stray;

H.

If, hapless chance! they linger lang,
 I'm scorching up sae shallow,
They're left the whitening stanes amang,
 In gasping death to wallow.

Last day I grat wi' spite and teen
 When Poet Burns came by,
That to a Bard I should be seen
 Wi' half my channel dry:
A panegyric rhyme, I ween,
 Even as I was, he shor'd me;
But had I in my glory been,
 He kneeling wad ador'd me. —

Here, foaming down the shelvy rocks,
 In twisting strength I rin;
There high my boiling torrent smokes
 Wild roaring o'er a linn:
Enjoying large each spring and well
 As Nature gives them me,
I am, altho' I say't mysel,
 Worth gaun a mile to see. —

Would

Would then my noble Master please
  To grant my highest wishes,
He'll shade my banks wi' towring trees
  And bonny spreading bushes:
Delighted doubly then, My Lord,
  You'll wander on my banks,
And listen mony a grateful bird
  Return You tuneful thanks. —

The sober laverock warbling wild
  Shall to the skies aspire;
The lairdie, Music's youngest child,
  Shall sweetly join the choir:
The blackbird strong, the lintwhite clear,
  The Mavis mild and mellow;
The Robin pensive Autumn chear,
  With all her locks of yellow: —

This too, a covert shall ensure
  To shield them from the storms,

                                        And

And coward Maukins sleep secure,
    Low in their grassy forms.
Here shall the shepherd make his seat,
    To weave his crown of flowers;
Or find a sheltering, safe retreat
    From prone-descending showers. —

And here, by sweet, endearing stealth,
    Shall meet the loving pair;
Despising worlds with all their wealth,
    As empty, idle care:
The flowers shall vie in all their charms
    The hour of heaven to grace;
And birks extend their fragrant arms
    To screen the dear embrace. —

Here haply too, at vernal dawn,
    Some musing Bard may stray;
And eye the smoking, dewy lawn,
    And misty mountain grey
Or, by the Reaper's nightly beam,
    Mild chequering thro' the trees,

Rave

Rave to my darkly-dashing stream,
    Hoarse-swelling on the breeze.

Let lofty firs and ashes cool,
    My lowly banks o'erspread,
And view, deep-bending in the pool,
    Their shadows' wat'ry bed:
Let fragrant birks in woodbines drest
    My craggy cliffs adorn,
And, for the little songster's nest
    The close embowering thorn. —

So may Old Scotia's darling hope,
    Your little angel band,
Spring, like their fathers, up to prop
    Their honor'd native land!
So may, thro' Albion's farthest ken,
    To social-flowing glasses
The grace be, — Athol's honest men,
    And Athol's bonie lasses!

God who knows all things, knows how my heart aches with the throes of gratitude whenever I recollect my reception at the noble house of Athole. —

Extempore Epistle to Mr. McAdam of Craigengillan, (wrote in Nanse Tinnock's Mauchline) in answer
to an obliging letter he sent, in the commencement of
my poetic career ——

Sir, o'er a gill I gat your card,
  I trow it made me proud; —
See wha taks notice o' the Bard!
  I lap and cry'd fu' loud. —

Now deil-ma-care about their jaw,
  The senseless, gauky million;
I'll cock my nose aboon them a',
  I'm roos'd by Craigengillan! ——

'Twas noble, Sir; 'twas like yoursel,
  To grant your high protection:
A Great man's smile ye ken fu' well,
  Is ay a blest infection. ——

Tho', by his* banes wha in a tub
  Match'd Macedonian Sandy!

_____

* Diogenes

On my ain legs thro' dirt I dub,
 I independant stand ay —
And when those legs to gude, warm hail,
 Wi' welcome canna bear me;
A lee dyke-side, a sybow-tail,
 And barley-scone shall cheer me. —

Heaven spare you lang to kiss the breath
 O' mony flowery Simmers!
And bless your bonie lasses baith,
 I'm tald they're loosome kimmers!

And God bless young Dunaskin's laird,
 The blossom o' our gentry!
And may he wear an auld man's beard,
 A credit to his country! —

On scaring some Water fowl in Loch-Turit, a
wild scene among the hills of Oughtertyre —

On scaring some Water fowl in Loch-Turit, a

    Why ye tenants of the lake, **Printed** ‖ 235
    For me your watry haunt forsake?
    Tell me, fellow creatures, why
    At my presence thus you fly?
    Why disturb your social joys
    Parent, filial, kindred ties?
    Common friend to you & me,
    Nature's gifts to all are free:
    Peaceful keep your dimpling wave,
    Busy feed, or wanton lave;
    Or beneath the sheltering rock,
    Bide the surging billows shock. —

    Conscious blushing for my kind,
    Soon, too soon your fears I find,
    Man, your proud, usurping foe,
    Would be lord of all below.

                 Plumes

Plumes himself in freedom's pride,
Tyrant stern to all beside.

Th' eagle from his cliffy brow,
Marking you his prey below;
In his breast no pity dwells,
Strong Necessity compels.
But man, to whom alone is given
A ray direct from pitying Heaven,
Glories in his heart humane —
And creatures for his pleasures slain.

In their savage, liquid plains,
Only known to wandering swains,
Where the mossy rivulet strays,
Far from human haunts & ways;
All on Nature you depend,
And life's poor season peaceful spend.
Or if Man's superiour might
Dare invade your native right,

On the lofty ether borne,
Man with all his powers you scorn:
Swiftly seek on clanging wings,
Other lakes and other springs;
And that foe you cannot brave,
Scorn at least to be his slave. ———

⟨flourish⟩

This was the production of a solitary forenoon's walk
from Oughtertyre-house. — I lived there, Sir William's
guest, for two or three weeks, & was much flattered by
my hospitable reception. — What a pity that the mere
emotions of gratitude are so impotent in this world!
'Tis lucky that, as we are told, they will be of some
avail in the world to come. ———

Printed 11 238

Written in the Hermitage at Taymouth. —

Admiring Nature in her wildest grace
These northern scenes with weary feet I trace;
O'er many a winding dale & painful steep,
Th' abodes of cover'd Grouse & timid sheep,
(My savage journey curious I pursue,
Till fam'd Breadalbine opens on my view. —
The meeting cliffs each deep-sunk glen divides,
The Woods wild-scatter'd clothe their towering sides;
Th' outstretching lake, embosom'd 'mong the hills,
The eye with wonder and amazement fills:
The Tay meandering sweet in infant pride,
The Palace rising on his verdant side;
The lawns wood-fring'd in Nature's native taste,
The hillocks dropt like Nature's careless haste;
The Arches striding o'er the new-born stream,
The Village glittering in the noontide beam. —

+ —

Poetic

Poetic ardours in my bosom swell,
Lone wand'ring by the hermit's mossy cell:
The sweeping theatre of hanging woods,
Th' incessant roar of headlong, tumbling floods —

+ + + + + + + + + + + + + + + + + +

Here Poesy might wake her heaven-taught lyre,
And look thro' Nature with creative fire;
Here, to the wrongs of Fate half reconcil'd,
Misfortune's lighten'd steps might wander wild;
And Disappointment in these lonely bounds,
Find balm to soothe her bitter rankling wounds,
Her heart-struck grief might heaven-ward
        stretch her scan,
And injur'd Worth forget and pardon Man. —

I wrote this with my pencil over the chimney piece
in the parlour of the Inn at Kenmore, at the outlet of Loch
Tay. —

Written at the Fall of Fyers —

Among the heathy hills and ragged woods,
The roaring Fyers pours his mossy floods;
Till full he dashes on the rocky mounds,
Where thro' a shapeless breach his stream resounds.
As high in air the bursting torrents flow,
As deep recoiling surges foam below:
Prone down the rock the whitening sheet descends
And viewless Echo's ear astonish'd rends:
Dim-seen thro' rising mists & ceaseless showers,
The hoary cavern wide-surrounding lowers:
Still thro' the gap the struggling river toils,
And still below the horrid caldron boils.

+ —

I composed these lines standing on the brink of the hideous
caldron below the water-fall.—

Written by Somebody on the window of an inn
at Stirling on seeing the Royal Palace in ruins.

Here Stewarts once in triumph reign'd,
And laws for Scotland's weal ordain'd;
But now unroof'd their Palace stands,
Their sceptre's fall'n to other hands;
Fallen indeed, and to the earth,
Whence grovelling reptiles take their birth.—
The injur'd Stewart-line are gone,
A Race outlandish fill their throne;
An idiot race, to honor lost;
Who know them best despise them most.

These imprudent lines were answered very petulantly
by somebody, I believe a Rev.ᵈ Mr. Hamilton.—In a M.S.S. where
I met with the answer, I wrote below—
With Esop's lion, Burns says, sore I feel
Each other blow; but d—mn that ass's heel !

Epistle to Robt. Graham Esq: of Fintry on the Elect.
for the Dumfries string of Boroughs, Anno 1790. ——

Fintry, my stay in worldly strife,
Friend o' my Muse, Friend o' my Life,
    Are ye as idle's I am?
Come then, wi' uncouth, kintra fleg,
O'er Pegasus I'll fling my leg,
    And ye shall see me try him. ——

I'll sing the zeal Drumlanrig bears,
Wha left the all-important cares
    Of fiddles, wh-res & hunters;
And, bent on buying Borough-towns,
I am shaking hands wi' wabster-louns,
    And kissen barefit bunters. ——

Confusion thro' our Boroughs rode,
Whistling his roaring pack abroad
    Of mad, unmuzzled lions;
As Queensberry Buff & Blue unfurled,
And Westerha & Hopeton hurled
    To every whig defiance. ——

But cautious Queensberry left the war,
Th' unmanner'd dust might soil his star,
    Besides, he hated Bleeding

But left behind him heroes bright,
  Heroes in Cæsarean fight,
    Or Ciceronian pleading. —

O for a throat like huge Monsmeg,
  To muster o'er each ardent Whig,
    Beneath Drumlanrig's banner!
Heroes & heroines commix,
All in the field of Politics
  To win immortal honor. —

M'murdo & his lovely Spouse,
  (Th'enamour'd laurels kiss her brows)
    Led on the Loves & Graces:
She won each gaping Burgess' heart,
  While he, sub rosa, play'd his part
    Among their wives & lasses. —

Craigdarroch led a light-arm'd Core,
  Tropes, metaphors & figures pour
    Like Hecla streaming thunder:
Glenriddel, skill'd in rusty coins,
  Blew up each Tory's dark designs,
    And bar'd the treason under. —

In either wing two champions fought;
  Redoubted Staig, who set at nought
    The wildest savage Tory:

                              While

83. While Welsh, who never flinch'd his ground,
   High-wav'd his magnum bonum round
     With Cyclopean fury. ——

Miller brought up th' artillery ranks,
The many pounders of the banks,
    Resistless desolation !
While Maxwelton, that baron bold,
'Mid LAWSON's port entrench'd his hold,
    And threaten'd worse damnation. ——

To these what Tory hosts oppos'd,
   With these what Tory warriors clos'd,
     Surpasses my descriving ;
Squadrons, extended long & large,
   With headlong speed rush to the charge,
     Like furious devils driving. ——

What Verse can sing, or Prose narrate,
The butcher deeds of bloody Fate,
    Amid this mighty tulzie !
Grim Horror girn'd; pale Terror roar'd,
As Murder at his thrapple shor'd,
    And Hell mix'd in the brulzie. ——

As Highland craigs by thunder cleft,
When lightenings fire the stormy lift,
    Hurl down wi' crashing rattle;

As flames among a hundred woods,
As headlong foam a hundred floods;
   Such is the rage of battle — .

Thy stubborn Tories dare to die;
As soon the rooted oaks would fly
   Before th' approaching fellers:
The Whigs come on like ocean's roar,
When all his wintry billows pour
   Against the Buchan bullers. —

Lo, from the shades of Death's deep night,
Departed Whigs enjoy the fight,
   And think on former daring:
The muffled Murtherer of Charles‡   {Charles 1st was executed
The Magna charta flag unfurls,   ‡ by a man in a mask. —
   All deadly gules it's bearing. —

Nor wanting ghosts of Tory fame;
Bold Scrimgeour‡ follows gallant Graham,‡   {‡ Viscount Dundee
   Auld Covenanters shiver!   ‡ Montrose —
Forgive, forgive! much-wrong'd Montrose!
  Now, Death & Hell engulph thy foes,
   Thou liv'st on high for ever.)

Still o'er the field the combat burns,
The Tories, Whigs, give way by turns,
   But Fate the word has spoken:
                       For

65 For Woman's wit, & strength of Man,
　　Alas! can do but what they can,
　　　The Tory ranks are broken. ——

　　O, that my een were flowing burns!
　　My voice, a lioness that mourns
　　　Her darling cub's undoing!
　　That I might greet, that I might cry,
　　While Tories fall, while Tories fly
　　　From furious whigs pursuing. ————

　　What Whig but melts for good Sir James!
　　Dear to his Country by the names,
　　　Friend, Patron, Benefactor!
　　Not Pulteney's wealth can Pulteney save;
　　And Hopeton falls, the generous, brave;
　　　And Stewart bold as Hector!

　　Thou, Pit, shalt rue this overthrow,
　　And Thurlow growl a curse of woe,
　　　And Melville melt in wailing:
　　How Fox & Sheridan rejoice!
　　And Burke shall shout—O Prince, arise!
　　　Thy power is all-prevailing!

O for your poor friend, the Bard, afar,
  He hears & sees the distant war,
    A cool spectator purely:
So, when the storm the forest rends,
O The Robin in the hedge descends,
    And patient chirps securely. ———

Now, for my friends' & brethren's sakes,
And for my native Land-o'-Cakes,
    I pray with holy fire;
Lord, send a rough-shod troop o' hell,
O'er a'; wad Scotland buy, or sell,
    And grind them in the mire!!!

          I am, &c.

          ⸺⸺⸺

87 = A Poet's welcome to his " love-begotten daughter „ the first instance that entitled him to the venerable appellation „ of „ Father. ——

MSS 2 fo 279

O Thou's welcome, Wean! Mischanter fa' me,
If thoughts o' thee, or yet thy Mamie,
Shall ever daunton me or awe me,
          My bonie lady;
Or if I blush when thou shalt ca' me
          ~~Tyta~~ or Daddie.

Tho' now they name me, Fornicator,
And tease my name in kintra clatter,
The mair they talk, I'm kend the better;
          E'en let them clash!
An auld wife's tongue's a feckless matter
          To gie ane fash. ——

Welcome! My bonie, sweet, wee Dochter!
Tho' ye come here a wee unsought for,
And tho' your comin I hae fought for,
          Baith Kirk & Queir,
Yet by my faith, ye're no unwrought for,
          That I shall swear!

Thou image o' my bonie Betty,
As fatherly I kiss & daut thee,

As dear & near my heart I set thee,
        Wi' as gude will,
As a' the Priests had seen me get thee
        That's out o' h—— ——

Sweet fruit o' monie a' merry dint,
My funny toil is no a' tint;
Tho' ye come to the warld asklent,
        Which fools may scoff at,
In my last plack your part's be in't
        The better half o't. ——

Tho' I should be the waur bestead,
Thou's be as braw & bienly clad,
And thy young years so nicely bred
        Wi' education,
As ony brat o' Wedlock's bed
        In a' thy station. ——

For if thou be, what I wad hae thee,
And tak the counsel I shall gie thee,
I'll never rue my trouble wi' thee,
        The cost nor shame o't,
But be a loving Father to thee,
        And brag the name o't. ——

89 The five Carlin's — A Ballad:—

MSS v 2 fo 287

There was five Carlins in the South,
  They fell upon a scheme,
To send a lad to London town,
  To bring them tidings hame. —

Not only bring them tidings hame,
  But do their errands there;
And aiblins gowd & honor baith
  Might be that laddie's share. —

There was, Maggy by the banks o' Nith,
  A dame wi' pride eneugh;
And Marjory o' the mony lochs,
  A Carlin auld & teugh:

And Blinkin Bess of Annandale,
  That dwalt near Solway-side;
And Brandy Jean that took her gill
  In Galloway sae wide:

And Black Joan frae Crighton-peel,
  O' gipsey kith & kin:
Five wighter Carlins were na found
  The South Coontrie within. — —

To send a lad to London town,
    They met upon a day;
And mony a Knight, & mony a Laird,
    That errand fain wad gae. —

O mony a Knight & mony a Laird,
    That errand fain wad gae;
But nae ane could their fancy please,
    O ne'er a ane but tway. —

The first ane was a belted Knight,
    Bred of a Border-band,
And he wad gae to London town,
    Might nae man him withstand. —

And he wad do their errands weel,
    And meikle he wad say;
And ilka ane at London court
    Wad bid to him gude-day. —

The niest ane was a Sodger-boy,
Wha ~~And~~ spak wi' modest grace;
And he wad gae to London town,
    If sae their pleasure was. —

He wad na hecht them courtly gifts,
  Nor meikle speech pretend;
But he wad hecht an honest heart,
  Wad ne'er desert his friend. ———

Now wham to chuse & wham refuse,
  At strife this Carlins fell;
For some had gentle folk to please,
  And some wad please themsel'. ———

Then out spak, mim-mou'd Meg o' Nith,
  And she spak out wi' pride,
And she wad send the Sodger-boy,
  Whatever might betide. ———

For th' Auld Gudeman o' London court,
  She did na care a pin;
But she wad send the Sodger-boy
  To greet his eldest son.. ———

Then upsprang Bess of Annandale,
  A deadly aith she's taen,
That she wad vote the Border Knight,
  Tho' she should vote her lane:

For far-off fowls: hae feathers fair,
    And fools o' change are fain;
But I hae try'd this Border Knight,
    I'll try him yet again.——

Then Brandy Jean spak o'er her drink,
    Ye weel ken, kimmers a',
The auld gudeman o' London court,
    His back's been at the wa':

And mony a friend that kiss'd his caup,
    Is now a fremit wight;
But its ne'er be sae wi' Brandy Jean,
    We'll send the Border Knight ——

Says Black Joan frae Crighton-peel,
    A Carlin stoor & grim,
The Auld gudeman, or the Young gudeman,
    For me may sink or swim:

For fools will prate o' Right & Wrang,
    While knaves laugh them to scorn;
But the Sodger's friends hae blawn the best,
    So he shall bear the horn.——

                                Then

O Then slaw rase Marjory o' the lochs,
    And wrinkled was her brow;
Her ancient weed was russet gray,
    Her auld Scots heart was true. —

O There's some Great Folk set light by me,
    I set as light by them.
But I will send to London town,
    Wham I loe best at hame. —

O Then how this weighty plea may end,
    Nae mortal wight can tell:
God grant, the King, & Ilka man,
    May look weel to himsel!

Extempore nearly —
On the birth of Mons.! Henri, posthumous child to a Mons.! Henri
a gentleman of family & fortune from Switzerland; who died
in three days illness, leaving his lady, a sister of Sir Tho.! Wallace,
in her sixth month of this her first child. ——— ○The
Lady & her ○Family were particular friends of the Author —
○The child was born in November —— 90 —

Printed || 243

Sweet ○Floweret, pledge o' meikle love,
 And ward o' mony a prayer,
That heart o' stane wad thou na move,
 Sae helpless, sweet & fair ———

November hirples o'er the lea,
 Chill on thy lovely form;
And gane, Alas! the sheltering tree,
 Should shield thee frae the storm. ——

May He, wha gies the rain to pour,
 And wings the blast to blaw,
Protect thee frae the driving shower,
 The bitter frost & snaw!

May He, the friend of woe & want,
 Who heals life's various stounds,

11

105. Protect & guard the Mother-Plant,
    And heal her cruel wounds. ——

But late she flourish'd, rooted fast,
    Fair on the summer morn;
Now feebly bends she in the blast,
    Unshelter'd & forlorn. ——

Blest be thy bloom, thou lovely gem!
    Unscath'd by ruffian hand!
And from thee many a Parent-stem
    Arise to deck our Land!

Birthday Ode — 31st Decemr 1787. —

Afar th' illustrious Exile roams,
   Whom kingdoms on this day should hail:
An inmate in the casual shed,
On transient pity's bounty fed,
Haunted by busy memory's bitter tale!
   Beasts of the forest have their savage homes;
   But He who should imperial purple wear,
Owns not the lap of earth where rests his royal head!

   His wretched refuge, dark despair,
   While ravening wrongs & woes pursue;
   And, distant far the faithful few
   Who would his sorrows share. —

   False flatterer, hope, away!
Nor think to lure us as in days of yore:
   We solemnize this sorrowing natal day,
To prove our loyal truth — we can no more;
   And owning Heaven's mysterious sway,
   Submissive, low, adore. —

Pye

Ye honored, mighty Dead!
Who nobly perished in the glorious cause,
Your King, your Country and her laws!
From great Dundee, who smiling Victory led,
And fell a martyr in her arms,
(What breast of northern ice but warms!)
To bold Balmerino's undying name,
Whose soul of fire, lighted at Heaven's high flame,
Deserves the proudest wreath departed heroes claim:
Not unrevenged your fate shall lie,
It only lags, the fatal hour;
Your blood shall with incessant cry.
Awake at last th' unsparing Power,
As from the cliff, with thundering course,
The snowy ruin smokes along,
With doubling speed, and gathering force,
Till deep it, crashing, whelms the cottage in the vale,
So Vengeance' arm, ensanguined, strong,
Shall with resistless might assail:
Usurping B——ch's pride shall lowly lay,
And Stewart's wrongs & yours, with tenfold weight, repay.

Perdition, baleful child of night!
Rise and revenge the injured right
Of St—w—rts' royal race:
Lead on the unmuzzled hounds of hell,
Till all the frighted echoes tell
The blood-notes of the chace!
Full on the quarry point their view,
Full on the base usurping crew,
The tools of faction, and the nation's curse!
Hark, how the cry grows on the wind,
They leave the lagging gale behind;
Their savage fury, pitiless, they pour;
With murdering eyes already they devour:
See B———ck spent, a wretched prey;
His life one poor despairing day,
Where each avenging hour still ushers in a worse!
Such havock, howling all abroad,
Their utter ruin bring;
The base apostates to their God,
Or rebels to their King.

Printed 11 Mrs Oswald of Auchencruive.
1,64

Ode sacred to the memory of Mrs O— of A.—w.

Dweller in yon dungeon dark,
Hangman of creation, mark!
Who in widow weeds appears,
Laden with unhonored years,
Noosing with care a bursting purse,
Baited with many a deadly curse?

Strophe

View the withered Beldam's face,
Can thy keen inspection trace
Aught of Humanity's sweet, melting grace?
Note that eye, 'tis rheum o'erflows,
Pity's flood there never rose;
See those hands ne'er stretched to save,
Hands that took, but never gave. —

Keeper of Mammon's iron chest,
Lo, there she goes, unpitied, & Unblest;
She goes, but not to realms of everlasting rest!

Pindarick

Antistrophe

Plunderer of Armies, lift thine eyes,
(A while forbear, ye torturing fiends,)
Seest thou whose step, unwilling, hither bends?
No fallen Angel, hurled from upper skies:
'Tis thy, trusty, quondam Mate;
Doomed to share thy fiery fate,
She, tardy, hellward plies. —

Epode

And are they of no more avail,
Ten thousand glittering pounds a year?
In other worlds can Mammon fail,
Omnipotent as he is here?
O bitter mockery of the pompous bier,
While down the wretched Vital-part is driven!
The cave lodged beggar, with a conscience clear,
Expires in rags, unknown, & goes to Heaven.

Extempore — to Mr Gavin Hamilton —

To You, Sir, this Summons I've sent,
  Pray whip till the Pownie is freathing;
But if you demand what I want,
  I honestly answer you Naething. —

Ne'er scorn a poor Poet like me
  For idly just living & breathing,
While people of every degree
  Are busy employ'd about — Naething. —

Poor Centum per centum may fast,
  And grumble his hurdies their claithing;
He'll find when the balance is cast,
  He's gane to the devil for — Naething. —

The Courtier cringes and bows,
  Ambition has likewise its plaything;
A Coronet beams on his brows,
  And what is a Coronet? naething.

Some quarrel the Presbyter gown,
  Some quarrel Episcopal graithing;

But

But every good fellow will own,
   Their Quarrel is all about—Naething.—

The lover may sparkle and glow,
   Approaching his bonie bit gay thing;
But marriage will soon let him know,
   He's gotten a buskit up a Naething.—

The Poet may jingle and rhyme,
   In hopes of a laureate wreathing
And when he was wasted his time,
   He's kindly rewarded with Naething.—

The thundering bully may rage,
   And swagger & swear like a heathen;
But collar him fast, I'll engage
   You'll find that his courage is Naething.—

Last night with a feminine Whig,
   A Poet she could na put faith in
But soon we grew lovingly big,
   I taught her, her terrors were—Naething.—

                   Her

Her whigship was wonderful pleased,
    But charmingly tickled wi' ae thing;
Her fingers I lovingly squeezed,
    And kissed her & promised her Naething. —

The Priests Anathemas may threat,
    Predicament, Sir, that we're baith in;
But when honor's reveillé is beat,
    The holy Artillery's — Naething. —

And now I must mount on the wave,
    My Voyage perhaps there is death in;
But what of a watery grave)!
    The drowning a Poet is Naething. —

And now as grim death's in my thought,
    To You, Sir, I make this bequeathing:
My service as lang as ye've ought,
    And my friendship, by G—d, when
        ye've Naething.

Lament of Mary Queen of Scots. —

Printed II 177

1

Now Nature hangs her mantle green,
      On every blooming tree;
And spreads her sheets o' daisies white,
      Out o'er the grassy lea:
Now Phebus chears the crystal streams,
      And glads the azure skies;
But nought can glad the weary wight
      That fast in durance lies. —

2.

Now laverocks wake the merry morn,
      Aloft on dewy wing;
The Merle in his noontide bower,
      Makes woodland echoes ring;
The Mavis mild, wi' mony a note,
      Sings drowsy day to rest;
In love and freedom they rejoice,
      Wi' care nor thrall opprest. —

Now

3.

Now blooms the lily by the bank,
  The primrose down the brae;
The hawthorn's budding in the glen,
  And milk-white is the slae:
The meanest hind in fair Scotland
  May rove their sweets among;
But I, the Queen of a' Scotland,
  Maun lie in prison strong. ——

4.

I was the Queen o' bonie France,
  Where happy I hae been;
Fu' lightly rose I in the morn,
  As blythe lay down at e'en:
And I'm the Sovereign of Scotland,
  And mony a traitor there;
Yet here I lie in foreign bands,
  And never-ending care. ——

But

5.

But as for thee, thou false Woman,
My Sister and my Fae;
Grim Vengeance yet shall whet a sword
That thro' thy soul shall gae!
The weeping blood in Woman's breast
Was never known to thee;
Nor the balm that drops on wounds of woe
Frae Woman's pitying eye!

6.

My Son, My son, may kinder Stars
Upon thy fortune shine!
And may those pleasures gild thy reign
That ne'er wad blink on mine!
God keep thee frae thy Mother's faes,
Or turn their hearts to thee!
And where thou meets thy Mother's friend,
Remember him for me!

7

O soon, to me, may Summer-Suns
Nae mair light up the morn;
Nae mair the winds of Autumn wave
Across the yellow corn!
And in the narrow house of Death
Let Winter round me rave;
And the next flowers that deck the Spring
Bloom o'er my peaceful grave!

Epistle to Robt. Graham Esqr. of Fintray
requesting a favor —

Mss v 1 to 587

When Nature her great Masterpiece designed,
And framed her last, best work, the Human Mind,
Her eye intent on all the mazy Plan,
She forms of various stuff the various Man.
The Useful Many first, she calls them forth,
Plain, plodding Industry, & sober Worth:
Thence Peasants, Farmers, native Sons of Earth,
And Merchandise' whole Genus take their birth:
Each prudent Cit a warm existence finds,
And all Mechanics' many-aproned kinds. —
Some other, rarer Sorts are wanted yet,
The lead & buoy are needful to the Net. —
The caput mortuum of gross Desires,
Makes a material for mere Knights & Squires;
The martial Phosphorus is taught to flow,
She kneads the lumpish Philosophic dough,
Then

Then marks th' unyielding mass w:t grand Designs,
Law, Physics, Politics and deep Divines:
Last, the sublimer th' Aurora of the Poles
The flashing elements of Female Souls . —

The ordered System fair before her stood,
Nature, well-pleased, pronounced it very good;
Yet, ere she gave creating labor o'er,
Half-jest, she tryed one curious labor more . —

Some spumy, fiery, ignis-fatuus matter,
Such as the slightest breath of air might scatter,
With arch-alacrity, & conscious glee,
(Nature may have her whim as well as we);
Her Hogarth-art perhaps she meant to show it,
She forms the Thing, & christens it — a Poet . —

Creature, tho' oft th' prey of Care & Sorrow,
When blest to day, unmindful of tomorrow;
A being form'd t'amuse his graver friends
Admired & praised — and there the wages ends;

W

A Mortal quite unfit for Fortune's strife,
Yet oft the sport of all the ills of life;
Prone to enjoy each pleasure riches give,
Yet haply wanting wherewithal to live;
Longing to wipe each tear, to heal each groan,
Yet frequent all-unheeded in his own. —

But honest Nature is not quite a Turk,
She laugh'd at first, then felt for her poor Work:
Viewing the propless Climber of Mankind,
She cast about a standard-tree to find;
In pity for his helpless woodbine-state,
She clasp'd his tendrils round the truly Great:
A Title, and the only one I claim,
To lay stronghold for help on generous Graham. —

Pity the tuneful Muses' hapless train,
Weak, timid Landsmen on life's stormy main!
Their hearts no selfish, stern absorbent stuff
That never gives — tho' humbly takes enough;

The

The little Fate allows they share as soon;
Unlike sage, proverbed-Wisdom's hard-wrung boon:
The World were blest, did bliss on them depend,
Ah, that the Friendly e'er should want a Friend!

Let Prudence number o'er each sturdy son
Who life & Wisdom at one race begun,
Who feel by reason, & who give by rule,
(Instinct's a brute, & Sentiment a fool!)
Who make poor, "Will do" wait upon "I should;"
We own they're prudent — but who owns they're good?
Ye Wise Ones, hence! ye hurt the social eye;
God's image rudely etched on base alloy!
But come, ye who the Godlike pleasure know,
Heaven's attribute distinguished — to bestow,
Whose arms of love would grasp all human race;
Come, thou who givest with all a courtier's grace,
Friend of my life! (true patron of my rhymes)
Prop of my life! dearest hopes for future times.

Why

Why shrinks my Soul, half-blushing, half-afraid,
Backward, abashed, to ask thy friendly aid?
I know my need, I know thy giving hand,
I tax thy Friendship at thy kind command:
But there are such, who court the tuneful Nine,
Heavens, should the branded character be mine!
Whose Verse in manhood's pride sublimely flows,
Yet vilest reptiles in their begging Prose. —
Mark, how their lofty, independant spirit
Soars on the spurning wing of injured Merit!
Seek you the proofs in private life to find?
Pity, the best of Words should be but wind!
So to Heaven's gates the lark's shrill song ascends
But grovelling on the earth the carol ends. —
In all the clamorous cry of starving Want
They dun Benevolence with shameless front:
Oblige them, patronize their tinsel lays,
They persecute You all your future days. —

Ever

'er my poor soul such deep damnation stain,
My horny fist assume the plough again;
The pie-bald jacket, let me patch once more;
On eighteen pence a Week I've lived before. —
Tho' thanks to heaven! I dare even that last shift:
I trust meantime, my boon is in thy gift,
That plac'd by thee upon the wished for height,
Where Man & Nature fairer in her sight,
My Muse may imp her wing for some
     sublimer flight.

Jeremiah 15.th Ch. 10 V.

Ah, woe is me, my Mother dear!
   A man of strife ye've born me:
For sair contention I maun bear,
   They hate, revile & scorn me. —

I ne'er could lend on bill or band,
   That five per cent might blest me;
And borrowing, on the tither hand,
   The de'il a ane wad trust me. ——

Yet I, a coin-denied wight,
   By Fortune quite discarded
Ye see how I am, day & night,
   By lad & lass blackguarded. ——

125.

†From Clarinda + on Mr B—'s saying that he ha
"nothing else to do":——

Then first you saw Clarinda's charms
   That raptures in your bosom grew!
~~Your Heart beat~~ shut to love's alarms,
   But then—you'd nothing else to do.——

Apollo oft had lent his harp,
   But now 'twas strung from Cupid's bow;
You sung, it reach'd Clarinda's heart,
   She wish'd—you'd nothing else to do.——

Fair Venus smil'd, Minerva frown'd,
   Cupid observ'd, the arrow flew:
Indifference (ere a week went round)
   Shew'd—you'd had nothing else to do.——
Christmas eve?   Clarinda——

————————————————————————————

+ ○ This Lady was the Authoress of two Songs, Nos 18
& 190, in the 2d Vol. of Johnson's Scots Musical Museum

Answer to the foregoing — Extempore

When dear Clarinda, matchless fair
 First struck Sylvander's raptur'd view,
He gaz'd, he listen'd to despair,
 Alas! 'twas all he dar'd to do. —

Love, from Clarinda's heavenly eyes,
 Transfix'd his bosom thro' & thro';
But still in Friendship's guarded guise,
 For more the demon fear'd to do. —

That heart, already more than lost,
 The imp beleaguer'd all perdue;
For frowning Honor kept his post,
 To meet that frown he shrunk to do. —

His pangs the Bard refus'd to own,
 Tho' half he wish'd Clarinda knew!
But Anguish wrung th' unweeting groan —
 Who blames what frantic Pain must do?

That heart, where motely follies blend,
 Was sternly still to Honor true:

To

To prove Clarinda's fondest friend,
  Was what a Lover sure might do. —

The Muse his ready quill employ'd,
  No dearer bliss he could pursue;
That bliss Clarinda cold deny'd —
  "Send word by Charles how you do!" —

The chill behest disarm'd his muse,
  Till Passion all impatient grew:
He wrote, & hinted for excuse,
  "'Twas 'cause he'd nothing else to do." —

But by those hopes I have above!
  And by those faults I dearly rue!
The deed, the boldest mark of love,
  For thee that deed I dare to do! —

O, could the Fates but name the price,
  Would bless me with your charms & you,
With frantic joy I'd pay it thrice,
  If human art or power could do!

Then take, Clarinda, friendship's hand,
  (Friendship, at least, I may avow;)
                                        A.

And lay no more your chill command,
   I'll write, whatever I've to do. ——

                              Sylvander

129 On the death of the late Lord President Dundas

Lone on the bleaky hills, the straying flocks,
Shun the fierce storms among the sheltering rocks,
Down foam the rivulets, red with dashing rains,
The gathering floods burst o'er the distant plains;
Beneath the blast the leafless forests groan,
The hollow caves return a sullen moan —
Ye hills, ye plains, ye forests & ye caves,
Ye howling winds, & wintry-swelling waves,
Unheard, unseen, by human ear or eye,
Sad to your sympathetick glooms I fly,
Where to the whistling blast & waters' roar,
Pale Scotia's recent wound I may deplore. —

O heavy loss thy Country ill could bear!
A loss these evil days can ne'er repair!
Justice, the high vicegerent of her God,
Her doubtful balance ey'd & sway'd her rod;
Hearing the tidings of the fatal blow,
She sunk abandon'd to the wildest woe. —

Wrongs, injuries, from many a darksome den
Now gay in hope explore the paths of men. — See

See from his cavern grim Oppression rise,
And throw on Poverty his cruel eyes,
Keen on the helpless victim see him fly,
And stifle, dark, the feebly-bursting cry!—
Mark ruffian Violence, distain'd with Crimes,
Rousing elate in these degenerate times;
View unsuspecting Innocence a prey,
As guileful Fraud points out the erring way:
While subtle Litigation's pliant tongue
The life-blood equal sucks of Right & Wrong.—
Hark, injur'd Want recounts th' unlisten'd tale,
And much-wrong'd Misery pours th' unpitied wail!

Ye dark, waste hills, ye brown, unsightly plains,
Congenial scenes! ye soothe my mournful strains:
Ye tempests, rage; ye turbid torrents, roll;
Ye suit the joyless tenor of my soul:
Life's social haunts & pleasures I resign,
Be nameless wilds & lonely wanderings mine,
To mourn the woes my Country must endure,
That wound degenerate ages cannot cure.—

131 The Whistle — A Ballad ——

Printed. II 247.

I sing of a whistle, a whistle of worth,
I sing of a Whistle the pride of the North,
Was brought to the court of our good Scotish king,
And long with this whistle all Scotland shall ring. —

Old Loda still rueing the arm of Fingal
The god of the bottle sends down from his hall,
"This Whistle's your challenge — to Scotland get o'er,
"And drunk them to hell, Sir.' or ne'er see me more!"

Old Poets have sung, & old chronicles tell
What champions ventur'd, what champions fell;
The Son of great Loda was conqueror still,
And blew on the Whistle their requiem shrill. —

Till Robert, the lord of the Cairn & the Scaur,
Unmatch'd at the bottle, unconquer'd in war,
He drank his poor godship as deep as the sea,
No tide of the Baltic e'er drunker than he. —
Thus Robert, victorious the trophy has gain'd,
Which now in his House has for ages remain'd;

Till three noble chieftans, & all of his blood,
The jovial contest again have renew'd ——

Three joyous good fellows with hearts clear of flaw,
Craigdarroch, so famous for wit, worth & law;
And trusty Glenriddel, so vers'd in old coins;
And gallant Sir Robert, deep-read in old wines. ——
Craigdarroch began with a tongue smooth as oil,
Desiring Glenriddel to yield up the spoil.
Or else he would muster the heads of the Clan,
And once more in Claret try which was the man.
"By the gods of the Ancients!" Glenriddel replies,
"Before I surrender so glorious a prize,
I'll conjure the ghost of the great Rory More,†
And bumper his horn with him twenty times o'er!"

Sir Robert, a soldier, no speech would pretend,
But he ne'er turn'd his back on his foe — or his friend;
Said, toss down the Whistle the prize of the field,
And knee-deep in Claret he'd die or he'd yield. ——

To the Board of Glenriddel our heroes repair,
So noted for drowning of sorrow & care,

But

† See, Johnson's tour
through Scotland ——

133 But for WINE & for WELCOME not more known to fame,
Than the sense, wit & taste of a sweet lovely DAME. —

A Bard was selected to witness the fray,
And tell future ages the feats of the day;
A Bard who detested all sadness & spleen,
And wish'd that Parnassus a vineyard had been. —

The dinner being over, the claret they ply,
And every new cork was a new spring of joy,
In the bands of old Friendship & Kindred so set,
And the bands grew the tighter the more they were we[t]

Gay Pleasure ran riot as bumpers ran o'er,
Bright Phebus ne'er witness'd so joyous a corps,
And vow'd that to leave them he was quite forlor[n]
Till Cynthia hinted he'd find them next morn.

Six bottles a piece had well wore out the night
When gallant Sir Robert, to finish the fight,
Turn'd o'er in one bumper a bottle of red,
And swore 'twas the way that their ANCESTOR did.

Then worthy Glenriddel so cautious & sage,
No longer the warfare ungodly would wage;

A

134

high Ruling Elder to wallow in wine!
He left the foul business to folks less divine. —

The gallant Sir Robert fought hard to the end,
But who can with Fate & quart-bumpers contend?
Tho' Fate said, a hero should perish in light,
So uprose bright Phebus—& down fell the Knight.

Next uprose the Bard, like a Prophet in drink,
"Craigdarroch, thou'lt soar when Creation shall sink!
"But if thou would'st flourish immortal in rhyme,
Come——one bottle more——& have at the sublime!

"Thy LINE that have struggled for freedom with BRUCE,
"Shall heroes & patriots ever produce.
"So thine be the Laurel, & mine be the Bay,
"The field thou hast won, by yon bright god of Day!"

A new "Psalm" for the Chapel of Kilmarnock,[436]
on the thanksgiving day for his Majesty's recovery —

O, sing a new song to the Lo——!
   Make, all & every one
A joyful noise, ev'n for the king
   His Restoration. —

The sons of Belial in the land
   Did set their heads together;
Come, let us sweep them off, said they,
   Like an o'erflowing river —

They set their heads together, I say,
   They set their heads together: *
On right, & left, & every hand,
   We saw none to deliver. —

Thou madest strong two chosen Ones,
   To quell the Wicked's pride:
That young Man, great in Issachar
   The burden-bearing Tribe. —

             And

137 And him, among the Princes chief
      In our Jerusalem,
The Judge that's mighty in thy law,
      The Man that fears thy name.

Yet they, even they, with all their might,
      Began to faint & fail;
Even as two howling, ravening wolves
   & To dogs do turn their tail: ——

Th' Ungodly o'er the Just prevail'd,
      For so thou hadst appointed,
That thou might'st greater glory give
      Unto thine own Anhointed. ——

And now thou hast restor'd our State,
      Pity our kirk also,
For she by tribulations
      Is now brought very low! ——

Consume that High Place, Patronage,
      From off thine holy hill;
And in thy fury burn the book
      Even of that man, M°Gill. ——

Now hear our Prayer, accept our Song,
  And fight thy Chosen's battle:
We seek but little, L——, from thee,
  O Thou kens we get as little. ——

A Ballad:— On the heresy of D.r M.Gill in Ayr

Orthodox, Orthodox, wha believe in John Knox,
  Let me sound an alarm to your conscience;
A heretic blast has been blawn in the West,
  "That what is not sense must be Nonsense."

+Doctor Mac, Doctor Mac, ye should streek on a rack,
  To strike evil-doers wi' terror:
To join Faith & Sense, upon any pretence,
  Was heretic, damnable error.———

+Dalrymple mild, Dalrymple mild, tho' your heart's like a ch
  And your life like the new-driven snaw;
Yet that winna save ye, auld Satan maun have ye,
  For preaching that Three's ane and twa!———

Calvin's sons, Calvin's sons, sieze your spiritual guns
  Ammunition ye never can need;
Your hearts are the stuff will be Powder enough,
  And your sculls are a storehouse of Lead.

——— + Doctor M.Gill, Ayr ———
+ D.r Dalrymple, Ayr ———

Rumble John, Rumble John, mount the steps with a groan,
    Cry, the book is with heresy cramm';
Then lug out your ladle, deal brunstane like aidle,
    And roar every note o' the Damn'd ——

Simper James, Simper James, leave the fair Killie dames,
    There's a holier chace in your view:
I'll lay on your head that the Pack ye'll soon lead,
    For Puppies like you there's but few ——

Andrew Gowk, Andrew Gowk, ye may slander the Book,
    And the Book nought the waur, let me tell ye:
Ye're rich, & look big, but lay by hat & wig,
    And ye'll hae a calf's head o' sma' value ——

Poet Willy, Poet Willy, gie the Doctor a volley,
    Wi' your "Leiberty chain," & your wit:
O'er Pegasus' side ye ne'er laid a stride,
    Ye only stood by where he sh— ——

—————————————————————————

1st John Russel, Kilmarnock —— 2. Jas. McKindlay, Kilm:ck
3d. Dr. Andrew Mitchel, Monkton —— 4th Will:m Peebles in
Newton upon Ayr, a Poetaster, who, among many other
things, published an Ode on the Centenary of the Revolution in
which was this line—"And bound in liberty's endearing chain"——

141

1 Barr Steenie, Barr Steenie, what mean ye? what mean ye?
   If ye'll meddle nae mair wi' the matter,
Ye may hae some pretence, man, to havins & sense, man,
   Wi' people that ken you nae better. ——

2 Jamie Goose, Jamie Goose, ye hae made but toom roose
   O' hunting the wicked Lieutenant;
But the Doctor's your mark! for the Lo—d's holy Ark
   He has cooper'd & ca'd a wrang pin in. ——

3 Davie Rant, Davie Rant, wi' a face like a saunt,
   And a heart that wad poison a hog;
Raise an impudent roar, like a breaker lee-shore,
   Or the KIRK will be tint in a bog. ——

4 Daddy Auld, Daddie Auld, there's a tod in the fauld,
   A tod meikle waur than the Clerk;
Tho' ye do little skaith ye'll be in at the death,
   For if ye canna bite, ye can bark. ——

————————————
1 Stephen Young, Barr — 2 Jas Young in New Cumnr
who had lately been foiled in an ecclesiastic prosecution
against a Lieut.t Mitchel ——————— 3d Dav.d Grant, Ochil
4.th Will.m Auld, Mauchlin; for the Clerk, see, Holy Willie's p

Muirland Jock, Muirland Jock, whom the L—d made a rock,
   To crush Commonsense for her sins;
If Illmanners were Wit, there's no mortal so fit
   To confound the poor Doctor at ance. ———

Cesnock-side, Cesnock-side, wi' your turkey-cock pride,
   O' manhood but sma' is your share;
Ye've the figure, it's true, even your faes maun allow,
   And your friends dauna say ye hae Mair. ——

Poet Burns, Poet Burns, wi' your priest-skelping turns,
   Why desert ye your auld native shire?
Tho' your Muse is a gipsey yet were she even tipsey,
   She could ca' us hae waur than we are. ——

1st John Shepherd, Muirkirk ———
2d George Smith, Galston ———

'143 To Rob.t Graham Esq: of Fintry on receiving a
favor ———

I call no goddess to inspire my strains,
A fabled Muse may suit a bard that feigns
O Friend of my life! my ardent spirit burns,
And all the tribute of my heart returns,
For boons accorded, goodness ever new,
The gift still dearer as the Giver You. —

Thou Orb of day! thou other Paler Light!
And all ye many sparkling stars of night!
If aught that Giver from my mind efface;
If I that Giver's bounty e'er disgrace;
Then roll to me, along your wandering spheres
Only to number out a villain's years!

Written in a wrapper inclosing a letter to
Captⁿ Grose, to be left with Mr Cardonnel an
Antiquarian ————

Tune, Sir John Malcolm ————

Ken ye ought o' Captain Grose?
    Igo & ago ——
If he's amang his friends or foes?
    Iram coram dago. ——
Is he South, or is he North?
    Igo & ago ——
Or drowned in the river Forth?
    Iram coram dago ——
Is he slain by Highland bodies?
    Igo & ago ——
And eaten like a wether-haggis?
    Iram coram dago. ——
Is he to Abram's bosom gane?
    Igo & ago ——
Or haudin Sarah by the wame?
    Iram coram dago ————

                              Whate'er

45 Whate'er he be, the Lord be near him!
        Igo & ago —
As for the deil, he daur na steer him,
        Iram coram dago. —
But please transmit th'inclosed letter,
        Igo & ago —
Which will oblidge Your humble debtor,
        Iram coram dago. —
So may ye hae auld stanes in store,
        Igo & ago —
The very stanes that Adam bore; —
        Iram coram dago. —
So may ye get in glad possession,
        Igo & ago —
The coins o' Satan's Coronation!
        Iram coram dago. —

1 Fragment — On Glenriddel's Fox breaking his chain

+ 93

Thou, Liberty, thou art my theme,
Not such as idle Poets dream,
Who trick thee up a Heathen goddess
That a fantastic cap & rod has!
Such stale conceits are poor & silly;
I paint thee out, a Highland filly,
A sturdy, stubborn, handsome dapple,
As sleek's a mouse, as round's an apple,
That when thou pleasest can do wonders;
But when thy luckless rider blunders,
Or if thy fancy should demur there,
Wilt break thy neck er thou go further. —

These things premis'd, I sing a fox;
Was caught among his native rocks,
And to a dirty kennel chain'd,
How he his liberty regain'd. ————

Glenriddel, a Whig without a stain,
A Whig in principle & grain,

147 Couldst thou enslave a free-born creature,
   A native denizen of Nature?
How couldst thou with a heart so good,
(A better ne'er was sluic'd with blood)
Nail a poor devil to a tree,
   That ne'er did harm to thine or thee?

      The staunchest Whig Glenriddel was,
      Quite frantic in his Country's cause;
   And oft was Reynard's prison passing,
   And with his brother Whigs canvassing
   The Rights of Men, the Powers of Women,
      With all the dignity of Freemen. ————

         Sir Reynard daily heard debates
   Of Princes' kings' & Nations' fates;
   With many
   With rueful, bloody stories
   Of tyrants, Jacobites & tories:
   From liberty how angels fell,
      That now are galley slaves in hell;
      How Nimrod first the trade began
         Of binding Slavery's chains on man;
                                          He

How fell Semiramis, G-d damn her!
Did first with sacreligious hammer,
(All ills till then were trivial matters)
For Man dethron'd forge hen-peck fetters;
How Xerxes, that abandon'd tory,
Thought cutting throats was reaping glory,
Untill the stubborn Whigs of Sparta
Taught him great Nature's Magna charta;
How mighty Rome her fiat hurl'd,
Resistless o'er a bowing world,
And kinder than they did desire,
Polish'd mankind with sword & fire:
With much too tedious to relate,
Of Axient & of Modern date,
But ending still how Billy Pit,
(Unlucky boy!) with wicked wit,
Has gagg'd old Britain, drain'd her coffer,
As butchers bind & bleed a heifer. —

          Thus wily Reynard by degrees,
     In kennel listening at his ease,   suck'd

¹⁴I suck'd in a mighty stock of knowledge,
As much as some folks at a college. —
Knew Britain's rights & constitution,
Her aggrandizement, diminution,
How fortune wrought us good from 'evil,
Let no man then despise the devil,
As who should say, I ne'er can need him;
Since we to scoundrels owe our freedom. —

Lament for James Earl of Glencairn —

Printed II 188

The wind blew hollow frae the hills,
　By fits the sun's descending beam
Look'd on the fading, yellow woods
　That wav'd o'er Lugar's winding stream:
Beneath a craigy steep, a Bard,
　Laden with years & meikle pain,
In loud lament bewail'd his Lord,
　Whom death had all untimely 'ta'en. —

He lean'd him to an ancient aik,
　Whose trunk was mouldering down with years;
His locks were bleached white by time,
　His hoary cheek was wet wi' tears:
And as he touch'd his trembling harp,
　And as he tun'd his doleful sang,
The winds lamenting thro' their caves,
　To echo bore the notes alang. —

"Ye scatter'd birds that faintly sing,
　The reliques o' the vernal queire;
Ye woods that shed on a' the winds
　The honors o' the aged year;

A

151 A few short ~~months~~ & glad & gay,
    Again ye'll charm the ear & 'e'e,
But nocht in all revolving time
    Can gladness bring again to me —

I am a bending, aged tree,
    That lang has stood the wind & rain,
And now has come a cruel blast,
    And my last hald of earth is gane:
Nae leaf o' mine shall greet the spring,
    Nae summer sun exalt my bloom;
But I ~~am~~ maun lie before the storm,
    And others plant them in my room.

I've seen sae mony changeful years,
    On earth I am a stranger grown;
I wander in the ways of men,
    Alike unknowing & unknown:
Unheard, unpitied, unreliev'd,
    I bear alane my lade o' care,
∞ For ~~him, low on beds of~~ ~~low lie a' in silent dust~~
    Lie a' that would my sorrows share —
And last, the sum of a' my griefs,
    My noble Master lies in clay;   The

 # For silent, low, on beds of dust

The flower amang our Barons bold
   His Country's pride, his Country's stay:
In weary being now I pine,
   For all the life o' life is dead,
And Hope has left my aged ken,
   On forward wing for ever fled. —

Awake thy last, sad voice, my harp,
   The voice of woe & wild despair;
Awake, resound my latest lay,
   Then sleep in silence evermair!
And thou, my last, best, only friend,
   That fillest an untimely tomb,
Accept this tribute from the Bard
   Thou brought'st frae fortune's mirkest gloom.
In Poverty's lone, barren vale
   Thick mists, obscure, involv'd me round;
Tho' oft I turn'd the wistful e'e,
   Nae ray o' fame was to be found:
Thou found'st me, like the morning sun
   That melts the fogs in limpid air;
The friendless Bard, & rustic song,
   Became alike thy fostering care. — O

O why has worth so short a date!
　　While villains ripen, grey, with time,
Must thou, the noble, gen'rous, great,
　　Fall in bald manhood's hardy prime!
Why did I live to see that day,
　　A day to me so full of woe!
O, had I met the mortal shaft
　　That laid my benefactor low!

The bridegroom may forget the bride,
　　Was made his wedded wife yestreen;
The monarch may forget the crown,
　　That on his head an hour has been;
The mother may forget the bairn
　　That smiles sae sweetly on her knee;
But I'll remember good Glencairn,
　　And a' that he has done for me.—

Epistle to Robert Graham Esq. of Fintry 5th Oct 1791

Printed II 181

Late crippled of an arm, & now a leg,
About to beg a pass for leave to beg,
Dull, listless, teazed, dejected & deprest,
(Nature is adverse to a cripple's rest)
Will generous Graham list to his Poet's wail?
(It soothes poor Misery, hearkening to her tale)
And hear him curse the light he first survey'd,
And doubly curse the luckless Rhyming trade.—

Thou, Nature, partial Nature, I arraign;
Of thy caprice maternal I complain.—
The lion & the bull thy care have found;
One shakes the forest, & one spurns the ground:
Thou givest the ass his hide, the snail his shell;
Th'envenomed wasp, victorious, guards his cell.—
Thy minions, kings, defend, control, devour,
In all th' omnipotence of rule & power.—
Foxes & statesmen, subtle wiles ensure;
The fit & polecat, stink, & are secure.—
Toads with their poison, doctors with their drug,
The priest & hedge hog in their robes, are snug.—
Even

155 Even silly women have defensive arts,
Their eyes, their tongues, & nameless other parts. —

But Oh, thou cruel stepmother & hard,
To thy poor, fenceless, naked child, the Bard !
A thing unteachable in worldly skill
And half an idiot too, more helpless still. —
No heels to bear him from the opening dun,
No claws to dig, his hated sight to shun:
No horns, but those by luckless Hymen worn,
And those, Alas! not Amalthea's horn:
No nerves olfactory, Mammon's trusty cur,
Clad in fat dullness' comfortable fur———
In naked feeling, & in aching pride,
He bears th' unbroken blast from every side:
Vampyre Booksellers drain him to the heart,
And Viper Critics cureless venom dart ! —

Critics, appalled I venture on the name,
Those cut-throat bandits in the paths of fame.—
Bloody dissecters, worse than ten Monroes;
He hacks, to teach; they mangle, to expose. —

'. His

His heart by wanton, causeless malice wrung;
By blockheads' daring into madness stung:
His well-won bays, than life itself more dear,
By miscreants torn who ne'er one sprig must wear:
Foiled, bleeding, tortured, in th' unequal strife,
The hapless Poet flounces on thro' life. —
Till fled each hope that once his bosom fired,
And fled each Muse that glorious once inspired;
Low sunk in squalid, unprotected age,
Dead, even resentment for his injured page,
He heeds, or feels no more the ruthless Critic's rage! }

So, by some hedge, the generous steed deceased,
For half-starved, snarling curs a dainty feast,
By toil & famine wore to skin & bone,
Lies senseless of each tugging bitch's son. —

O Dullness! Portion of the truly blest!
Calm, sheltered haven of eternal rest!
Thy sons ne'er madden in the fierce extremes
Of fortune's polar frost, or torrid beams —
If, mantling high, she fills the golden cup,
With sober, selfish ease they sip it up:
Conscious the bounteous meed they will deserve,
They only wonder "some folks" do not starve! — S. The

Lines to Sir John Whitefoord of Whitefoord, with the
Poem to the memory of Lord Glencairn —
See page 150. —

See page 150.

Printed II 194

O thou, who thy honor as thy God rever'st;
Who, save thy mind's reproach, nought earthly fear'st,
Witness the ardour of ~~this~~ votive lay,
With streaming eyes & throbbing heart I pray:—
The FRIEND thou valued'st, I, The Patron, lov'd:
His Worth, his HONOR, all the world approv'd.—
We'll mourn till we, too, go as he has gone,
And tread the shadowy path to that dark world unknown.—

157 The sage, grave-stern thus, easy, picks his frog,
And thinks the mallard a sad, worthless dog. —
When disappointment snaps the clue of hope,
And thro' disastrous night they darkling grope,
With deaf endurance sluggishly they bear,
And just conclude that "fools are fortune's care." —
So, heavy, passive to the tempest's shocks,
Strong on the sign-post stands the stupid ox. —

Not so the idle Muses' madcap train,
Nor such the workings of their moon-struck brain:
In equanimity they never dwell,
By turns in soaring heaven, or vaulted hell. —

I dread thee, Fate, relentless & severe,
With all a' Poet's, husband's, father's fear. —
Already one strong hold of hope is lost,
Glencairn the truly-noble lies in dust:
O, hear my ardent, grateful, selfish prayer!
Fintry, my other stay, long bless & spare!
Thro' a long life his Hopes & wishes crown,
And bright in cloudless skies his sun go down!
May bliss domestic smooth his private path,
Give energy to life, & soothe his latest breath
With many a filial tear circling the bed of death!

159 A Grace before dinner; Extempore!

O, thou, who kindly dost provide
  For every creature's want!
We bless thee, God of nature wide,
  For all thy goodness lent:
And, if it please thee heavenly guide,
  May never worse be sent;
But whether granted or denied
  Lord bless us with content!
        Amen!!!

Epigrams
On being asked why God had made Miss Davies so
little & Mrs —— so big —

  Ask why God made the gem so small,
    And why so huge the granite?
  Because God meant mankind should set
    That higher value on it ——

  On hearing it said that there was falsehood in
Dr B—b—ngton's very looks ——

  That there is falsehood in his looks
    I must & will deny:
  They say their master is a knave—
    And sure they do not lie. ——

  On Captn W—— Riddock of Corbeton Mss fo 308
Light lay the earth on Billy's breast
  His chicken heart so tender.
But build a castle on his head
  His scull will prop it under. —— .

On W— Gr—h—m esq: of M—ssfkn—w

"Stop thief!" dame Nature called to Death,
As Willie drew his latest breath
How shall I make a fool again—
My choicest model thou hast ta'en —

On Capt.n L—ss—ll—s —

When Lascelles thought fit from this world to depart,
Some friends warmly spoke of embalming his heart:
A bystander whispers, pray don't make so much on't,
The subject is poison—no reptile will touch it. —

Pinned to Mrs Walter Riddell's carriage

If you rattle along like your Mistress's tongue,
Your speed will outrival the dart:
But a fly for your load, you'll break down on the road
If your stuff be as rotten's her heart. —

Epitaph on John Bushby

Here lies John Bushby, honest man!
Cheat him devil — if you can. ———

———

On John M---r-ne, laird of L-gg-n ———

When M---r---ne, deceased, to the devil went down,
'Twas nothing would serve him but Satan's own crown:
Thy fool's head, quoth Satan, that crown shall wear never;
I grant thou'rt as wicked — but not quite so clever. ———

———

On the laird of C-rd-nn-ss

Bless J-s-s Chr-st, O C-rd-nn-ss,
    With grateful lifted eyes,
Who taught, that not the soul alone
    But body too shall rise.
For had he said, "the soul alone
    "From death I will deliver,"
Alas, alas, O C-rd-nn-ss,
    Then hadst thou lain for ever!

———

Contents of this Volume. " Page

At the end of the volume is inserted Mrs Wallace Currie's note announcing her presentation of the MS. to the Athenæum.

1- 2- 14 20 26 27 $\overline{21}$ 60 63 66

7 79 80 $\overline{8.1}$ $\overline{106}$ $\overline{111}$

124 125 126 $\overline{136}$ 139

143 144 159 160 160

161 161 161 162 162

162

ATHENÆUM
LIVERPOOL.

2 1. 27- 81- 106 111 136

To The President
of the Athenæum
Liverpool

Ellerslie
Dec 6th 1853

Sir

Will you allow me to
make you the Medium
of presenting to the Athenæum
Library two Manuscript
Books, in his own writing,
Poems & Letters of Burns.
I believe they came into
possession of Dr Currie when
he was engaged in writing
the Life of the Poet; & I shall
feel gratified by their finding
a place in the Library of an
Institution in which he took
so great an Interest —
I am Sir.
Your Obedt Servt
S. Currie

THE
GLENRIDDELL MANUSCRIPTS
OF
ROBERT BURNS

VOLUME II
LETTERS

LETTERS BY

Mr BURNS

which he selected for Rt Riddell Esqr

of Glenriddell

F·A·S· of London & Edinr

and member of the Literary and

Philosophical Society at

MANCHESTER.

The whistle.

ROBERTUS BURNS SCOTUS.

ATHENÆUM
LIVERPOOL

(2)

(6)

The following Scots fragment I wrote, I think, from
article. sometime in 1787 to My Friend Nicol.—

Kind-hearted Willie,

                    I'm sitten down here, after
en & forty miles riding, as forjesket & forniaw't
a forfoughten cock, to gie you some notion of my
ndlowper-like stravaiguin, sin I shook hands,
parted wi' auld Reekie.—
My auld, ga'd gleyde of a Meere has
chyald up-hill & down-brae, in Scotland & England,
teugh & birnie as a vera deevil wi' me.—
's true, she's as poor's a sang-maker, & as
rd's a Kirk; & tipper-taipers when she taks
gate first, like a lady's gentlewoman in a
inuwae, or a hen on a het girdle; but she's
noble, pouthery: girran for a' that; & has a
mack like Willie Stalker's Meere that wad hae
gested tumbler-wheels, for she'll whip me off
                                                her

her five stimparts [8] o' the best aits at a dow
sitting, & ne'er fash her thumb. —— When a
her ringbanes & spavies, her cruicks & crampo
are fairly soupl't, she beets to, beets to, & ay th
hindmost hour the tightest. — I could wager
price (& that, ye ken, was odds o' faur hund ster
to a thretty pennies, that for a fortnight's ryde
at fifty mile a day, the deil sticket a five gallo
acquesh Clyde & Whitehorn could cast saut in
her tail. ————   + + + -< m

The following was to one of the most accomplished of sones of men that I ever met with— John Arnot Dalquhatswood in Ayr-shire— alas! had he been really prudent! —— It is a damning circumstance human-life, that Prudence, insular & alone, without other virtue, will conduct a man to the most envied eminences in life, while every other good quality, & having wanting that one, which at best is itself but half a virtue, will not save a man from the world's contempt, & real misery, perhaps perdition. —

The story of the letter was this — I had got deeply in love with a young Fair-One, of which proofs were every day arising more & more to view. — I would gladly have covered my Inamorato from the darts of Calumny with the conjugal shield, nay, had actually made up some sort of Wedlock; but I was at that time deep in the guilt of being unfortunate, which good & lawful objection, the Lady's friends broke all our measures, & drove me sans desspoir. —

think that the letter was written sometime about the latter end of 1785, as I was meditating to publish my Poems

To John Arnot of Dalquatswood Esquire, inclosing
subscription-bill for my first edition, which wa[s]
printed at Kilmarnock ———

Sir,

  I have long wished for some kind of clai[m]
to the honor of your acquaintance, & since it is o[ut]
of my power to make that claim by the least ser[vice]
of mine to you, I shall do it by asking a friendl[y]
office of you to me. — I should be much hurt, &[c.]
if any one should view my poor Parnassian Peg.
in the light of a spur-galled Hack, & think th[at]
I wish to make a shilling or two by him. — I
spurn the thought. —

  It may-do—maun-do, Sir, wi' them wha
Maun please the great folk for a warme-fou;
For me, sae laigh I need na bow
For, Lord be thankit. I can plough:
And when I downa yoke a naig
Then, Lord be thankit! I can beg ——

You will then, I hope Sir, forgive my troubling you
with the inclosed; & spare a poor, heart-crush[ed]
    devi[l]

...il, a world of apologies: a business he is very unfit
at any time, but at present, undoned as he is of
...ry woman-giving comfort, he is utterly incapable
...— Sad & grievous, of late, Sir, has been my tribulation,
many & piercing, my sorrows; & had it not been
...the loss the world would have sustained in losing
...great a Poet, I had, ere now, done as a much wiser
...an the famous Achitophel of long-headed memory,
...d before me, when "he went home & set his house
...order." —— I have lost, Sir, that dearest earthly
...save, that greatest blessing here below, that last, best
...t which compleated Adam's happiness in the
...rden of bliss, I have lost—I have lost—my trembling
...and refused its office, the frighted ink recoils
...the quill— Tell it not in Gath—I have lost—
...a—a Wife!

Fairest of god's creation, last & best!
Now art thou lost——

...u have doubtless, Sir, heard my story, heard it with
...l its exaggerations; but as my actions, & my motives
...action, are peculiarly like myself, & that is
...culiarly like nobody else, I shall just beg a
leisure

leisure-moment & a spare-tear of you, untill I tell
own story my own way. ——

    I have been all my life, Sir, one of the rueful
looking, long-visaged sons of Disappointment. —
A damned Star has always kept my zenith, &
shed its baleful influence, in that emphatic curse of th'
Prophet—"And behold, whatsoever he doth, it shall
"not prosper!". —— I rarely hit where I aim; &
if I want any thing, I am almost sure never to
find it where I seek it. — For instance, if my pen-
knife is needed, I pull out twenty things—a plou
-wedge, a horse-nail, an old letter or a tattered rhyme
in short, every thing but my pen-knife; & tha
at last, after a painful, fruitless search, will be
found in the unsuspected corner of an unsuspe
pocket, as if on purpose thrust out of the way
Still, Sir, I had long had a wishing eye to that inestim
blessing, a wife. — My mouth watered deliciously, to
a young fellow, after a few idle, common-place stories
from a gentleman in black, strip & go to bed with
a young girl, & no one durst say black was his eye
while I, for just doing the same thing, only war
                                          tha

t ~~insignificant~~ ceremony, am made a Sunday's laugh-
g stock, & abused like a pick-pocket. — I was well aware
ugh, that if my ill-starred fortune got the least hint
my connubial wish, my schemes would go to nothing.—
o prevent this, I determined to take my measures
th such thought & forethought, such caution & pre-
ution, that all the malignant planets in the Hemi-
here should be unable to blight my designs. —
F content with, to use the words of the celebrated Westminster
vines, "The outward & ordinary means," I left
o stone unturned; sounded every unfathomed
pth; stopped up every hole & bore of an objection:
t, how shall I tell it! notwithstanding all this turn-
g of stones, stopping of bores, &c. — whilst I, with secret
easure, marked my project swelling to the proper
sis, & was singing Te deum in my own fancy; or
change the metaphor, whilst I was vigourously
essing on the siege; had carried the counterscarp,
made a practicable breach behind the curtin in
gorge of the very principal bastion; nay, having
stered the covered way, I had found means to slip a
oice detachment into the very citadel; while I had
                                                    nothing

nothing lefs in view than displaying my victorious b[...]
ners on the top of the walls— Heaven & Earth, must [...]
"remember"! my damned star wheeled about to the Z[...]
by whose baleful rays Fortune took the alarm, & pour[...]
in her forces on all quarters, front, flank & rear, I wa[...]
utterly routed, my baggage lost, my military chest [...]
the hands of the enemy; & your poor devil of a hum[...]
servant, commander in chief forsooth, was obliged to scar[...]
away, without either arms or honors of war, except
bare bayonet & catridge-pouch; nor in all probability
he escaped even with them, had he not made a shi[...]
to hide them under the lap of his military cloak.

In short, Pharaoh at the Red Sea, Darius at Arbela,
Pey at Pharsalia, Edward at Bannockburn, Charles a[...]
Pultaway, Burgoyne at Saratoga—— no Prince, Pote[...]
or Commander, of ancient or modern unfortunat[...]
memory, ever got a more shameful or more tota[...]
defeat.— "O horrible! O horrible. Most horrible!

How I bore this, can only be conceived. —All po[...]
of recital labor far, far behind. — O there is a fir[...]

rge portion of bedlam in the composition of a Poet
any time; but on this occasion, I was nine parts &
ne tenths, out of ten, stark staring mad. — At first,
was fixed in stuporific insensibility, silent, sullen, staring,
he Lot's wife besaltified in the plains of Gomorrha. —
But my second paroxysm chiefly beggars description.—
e rifted northern ocean, when returning suns dissolve
e chains of winter, & loosening precipices of long
ccumulated ice tempest with hideous crash the foamy
eep — images like these may give some faint shadow
~~an idea~~ of what was the situation of my bosom. —
y chained ~~faculties~~ broke loose; my maddening passions, roused
ten-fold fury, bore over their banks with impetuous
istless force, carrying every check & principle before
em. — Counsel, was an unheeded call to the passing
rricane; Reason, a screaming alk in the ~~whirling~~
rtex of Moskoestrom; & Religion, a feebly-struggling
wer down the roarings of Niagara. — I reprobated
first moment of my existence; execrated Adam's
lly-infatuated wish for that goodly-looking, but poison-
eathing, gift, which had ruined him, & undone me;
called on the womb of uncreated night to close over
e & all my sorrows! —   A

A storm naturally overblows itself. — My after passions gradually sank into a lurid calm; & by de I have subsided into the time-settled sorrow of the sable widower, who, wiping away the decent tear, lifts up his grief=worn eye to look — for another wife. —

"Such is the state of man; today he buds
"His tender leaves of hope; tomorrow blossoms,
"And bears his blushing honors thick upon him;
"The third day comes a frost, a killing frost
"And nips his root, & then he falls as I do"

————"

Such, Sir, has been this fatal era of my life
"And it came to pass, that when I looked for sweet,
"behold bitter; & for light, behold darkness" —

But this is not all. — Already the holy beagles the houghmagandie pack, begin to snuff the scent & I expect every moment to see them cast off & hear them after me in full cry: but as I am an old fox, I sh give them dodging & doubling for it; & by & by I intend to earth among the mountains of Jamaica

I am so struck, on a review, with the impertinent length of this letter, that I shall not increase it with one single word of an apology; but abruptly conclude with assuring you, that I am,

Sir,

your, & Misery's most humble serv.t

In 1790, or 91 } To Charles Sharpe Esq: of Hoddam, und
a fictious signature, inclosing a ballad ———

copied for 2ᵈ Edit. —

vol 2 Nᵒ 87

It is true, Sir, you are a gentleman of rank & fortune, &
I am a poor devil: you are a feather in the cap of Society,
I am a very hobnail in his shoes; yet I have the honor
to belong to the same Family with you, & on that score
now address you. — You will perhaps suspect that I am
to claim affinity with the ancient & honorable House of
Kilpatrick? — No, no, Sir: I cannot indeed be proper
said to belong to any House, or even any province or
kingdom; as my mother, who for many years was sho
to a marching regiment, gave me into this bad world,
aboard the Packet-boat, somewhere between Donaghad
& Portpatrick. — By our common Family, I mean
Sir, the Family of the Muses. — I am a Fiddler
a Poet; & you, I am told, play an exquisite violin
& have a standard taste in the Belles Lettres.

The other day, a brother Cat-gut gave a charming
Scots air of your composition. — If I was pleased
we

...h the tune, I was in raptures with the title you have given it; & taking up the idea, I have spun it into the ...ee stanzas inclosed. — Will you allow me, Sir, to present ...n them, as the dearest offering that a misbegotten son ...Poverty & Rhyme has to give? — I have a [woman's] ...ging to take you by the hand, & unburthen my heart saying, "Sir, I honor you, as a man who supports the ...nity of Human-nature, amid an age when Frivolity & ...arice have between them, debased us below the brutes ...t perish!" — But, alas, Sir! to me you are unapp...roachable. —— It is true, the Muses baptized me ... Castalian-streams, but the thoughtless gipseys forgot to ...e me A NAME: —— As the Sep. have served many ...ood fellow; the Nine have given me a great deal of ...easure, but, bewitching jades! they have beggared me ...uld they but spare me a little of their cast-linen! ...e it only to put it in my power to say, that I have ...shirt on my back! — But the idle-wenches, like ...mon's lilies, "they toil not, neither do they spin," ...I must e'en continue to tie my remnant of a cravat ...e the hangman's rope, round my naked throat; ...oax my galligaskins to keep together their many-colo...fragments, & conceal with all their remaining strength

strength (a strength, alas, seldom equal to the task!) th
indecent efforts, & obscene exhibitions, of their unruly
inmate.) — As to the affair of shoes, I have given
up! — My pilgrimages in my ballad-trade, from town
to town, & on your stony-hearted turn-pikes too, a
what not even the hide of Job's Behemoth could bea
The coat on my back, is no more: I shall not speak e
of the dead. — It would be equally unhandsome & un
grateful, to find fault with my old surtout, which
kindly supplies & conceals the want of that coat. —
hat indeed is a great favorite; & though I got it lik
for an old song, I would not exchange it for the bes
beaver in Britain. — I was, during several year
a kind of fac-totum servant to a country clergym
where I pickt up a good many scraps of learning
particularly in some branches of the mathematics
Whenever I feel inclined to rest myself on my way
take my seat under a hedge, laying my poetic wall
on the one side, & my fiddle-case on the other; &
cing my hat between my legs, I can by means of
brim or rather brims, go through the whole doctr
of the Conic Sections —

Dowe

(2)

However, Sir, don't let me mislead you, as if I
would interest your pity. — Fortune has so much forsaken
me, that she has taught me to live without her; & amid
all my rags & poverty, I am as independant, & much
more happy, than a monarch of the world. — Accord-
ing to the hackneyed metaphor, I value the several
actors in the great Drama of life, simply as they act
their parts. — I can look on a worthless fellow of a Duke,
with unqualified contempt; & can regard an honest scavenger
with sincere respect. — As you, Sir, go through your
role with such distinguished merit, permit me to make
one in the chorus of universal applause, & assure you
that with the highest respect,

I have the honor to be &c. —

Fragment —. to my friend Cunningham of
a severe love-disappointment. —

My. Dear Sir,

〈When I saw in my last Newspaper
an account that a surgeon in Edin.r was married
a certain amiable & accomplished young lady whose
name begins with A——, a lady with whom I
fancy I have the honor of being a little acquain.
I, sincerely felt for you 〉— As you are the single or
instance in human-nature that ever came within
the sphere of my observation, of a young fellow,
dissipated but not debauched, a circumstance that
has ever given me the highest idea of the nati
qualities of your the native qualities of your hear.
I am certain that a disappointment in the tende
passion must, to you, be a very serious matter
To the hopeful youth, keen on the foot of Mamm
or listed under the gaudy banners of Ambition,
love-disappointment, as such, is an easy busine
nay, perhaps he hugs himself on his escape: b

your scanty tribe of mankind, whose souls bear on the best materials the most elegant impress of the Great Creator, Love enters deeply into their existence, & entwisted with their very thread of life. — I my-self can from experience affirm, that Love is the Alpha & Omega of human enjoyment. — All the Pleasures, all the happiness, of the Cottage, flow imme-diately & directly from this delicious source. — It is that spark of Celestial fire which lights up the wintry hut of Poverty, & makes the chearless mansion, warm comfortable & gay. — It is the emanation of Divinity, which preserves the sons & daughters of labor from degenerating into the brutes with which they daily would converse. — Without it, life, to my poor Com-ers, would be a damning gift. — + + + + +

+ + + + + + + + + + + + + + + + + + +

Q To M.rs Stewart of Stair: on the eve of my going No 2
Jamaica ———

34

Madam;

The hurry of my preparations for goi
abroad, has hindered me from performing my pro
mise so soon as I intended — I have here sent
you a parcel of Songs, &c. which never made their
appearance except to a friend or two at most —
The song is to the tune of Oltrick banks, you will
easily see the impropriety of exposing it much, ev.
in manuscript — I think myself it has some mer
both as a tolerable description of one of Nature's Swe
scenes, a July evening; & one of the finest pieces o
Nature's workmanship, the finest indeed we know
any thing of, an amiable beautiful young woma
but I have no common friend to procure me tha
permission, without which I would not dare to
the copy —
I am quite aware, Madam, what task the world i
assign me in this letter — The obscure Bard, wh
any of the Great condescend to take notice of him

...ould heap the altar with the incense of flattery. —
...eir high Ancestry, their own great & godlike qualities
...actions, should be recounted with the most exagge-
...ted description. — This, ~~task~~ Madam, is a task for
...ich, I am altogether unfit. — Besides a certain dis-
...alifying pride of heart; I know nothing of your
...nnections in life, & have no access to where your
...al character is to be found — the company of your.
...mpeers; & more, I am afraid that even the most
...fined adulation, is by no means the road to your
...d opinion. —

...ne feature of your character I shall ever with
...ateful pleasure remember, the reception I got
...hen I had the honor of waiting on you at Blair. —
...am little acquainted with politeness, but I know
...a good deal of benevolence of temper & goodness of
...art. — Surely, did those in exalted stations know
...w happy they could make some classes of their
...feriours by condescension & affability, they would
...ver stand so high; measuring out with every
...i the height of their elevation, but condescend as
...eetly as did Mrs S of St.

: A song I had written on Miss Wilhelmina Alexander
...f Ballochmyle — Vide, following letter —

To Miss P————————— J. Blacklock ~~smith~~

126 № 1

inclosing a song I had composed on her. ——

vol 1 pa 126

Madam

Poets are such outré beings, so much th
children of wayward fancy & capricious whim, t
I believe the world generally allows them a larger l
-titude in the rules of propriety, than the sober so
of Judgement & Prudence. —— I mention this a
an apology ~~all at once~~ for the liberties that a n
~~less~~ stranger has taken with you in the inclose
which he begs leave to present you ~~with~~. —— Wheth
it has poetical merit any way worthy of the
theme I am not the proper judge: but it is the
my abilities can produce; &, what to a good heart w
~~be~~ perhaps be a superiour grace, it is equally
sincere ~~or fervent~~.

The scenery was nearly taken from real life
though I dare say, Madam, you do not recollect it, a
believe you scarcely noticed the Poetic Reveur as
wandered by you. —— I had roved out as Chance
direc

vected, on the favorite haunts of my Muse, the banks
Ayr; to view Nature in all the gayety of the vernal
ar! — The sun was flaming o'er the distant, west-
n hills; not a breath stirred the crimson opening
ssom, or the verdant spreading leaf. — 'Twas a golden
oment for a Poetic heart. — I listened the feathered
arblers, pouring their harmony on every hand, with
ongenial, kindred regard; & frequently turned out of
y path, lest I should disturb their little songs, or frighten
m to another station. — "Surely," said I to myself, "he
ust be a wretch indeed, who, regardless of your harmo-
ious endeavours to please him, can eye your elusive
ights to discover your secret recesses & rob you of all
e property Nature gives you, your dearest comforts,
ur helpless nestlings!" — "Even the hoary hawthorn
ig that shot across the way, what heart as such a
me, but must have been interested in its welfare,
wished it to be preserved from the rudely browsing
ttle, or the withering eastern blast? — Such was the
ene, & such the hour, when, in a corner of my pros-
ct, I spied one of the finest pieces of Nature's work-
anship that ever crowned a Poetic landscape; those
sionary Bards excepted who hold commerce with
erial beings. — Had Calumny & Villainy taken
                                                        my

my walk, they had at that moment sworn eternal peace with such an Object. ———

What an hour of inspiration for a Poet! — It would have raised plain, dull, historic Prose to meta-phor & measure —

The inclosed song was the work of my return home; & perhaps but poorly answers what might have been expected from such a scene. — I am going to print a second edition of my Poems, but cannot insert these verses without your permission. —

I have the honor to be, Madam,

your most obedient & very humble servant

"Well Mr Burns, & did the Lady give you the desired "Permission?" — No! She was too fine a Lady to notice so plain a compliment. — As to her great brother whom I have since met in life, on more equal terms of respectability, why should I quarrel their want of attention to me? — When Fate swore that their purses should be full, Nature was equally positive that their heads should be empty. — "Men of their fashion were so "incapable of being unpolite?" — Ye canna mak a silk-purse o' a sow's

To Mr McmurDo at Drumlanrig, inclosing a
Song —

Sir

a Poet & a Beggar: are in so many points of
view alike, that one might take them for the same
individual character under different designations;
were it not that though, with a very trifling Poetic licence,
most Poets may be styled Beggars, yet the converse of
the proposition does not hold, that every Beggar is a
Poet. — In one particular however they remarkably
agree; if you help either the one or the other to a mug
of Ale, or the picking of a bone, they will very willingly
pay you with a song. — This occurs to me at present,
as I have just dispatched a well-lined rib of J. Rankine's
Highlander; a bargain for which I am, in the style of
our Ballad-printers, "Five excellent new songs" in
your debt. — The inclosed is nearly my newest
song, & one that has cost me some pains, though
that is but an equivocal mark of its excellence. —
Two or three others, I have by me, shall do themselves the honor of waiting to wait on you at
your after leisure: petitioners for favor admittance
to favor, must not harass the condescension of
                                                    their

their Benefactor. ————————

You see, Sir, what it is to patronize a Poet. —
'Tis like being a magistrate in a petty Borough: y
do them the favor to preside in their Council for on
year, & your name bears the prefatory stigma of
Bailie for life: —

I have the honor to be &c. ———————

On rummaging over some old papers, I lighted on
M.S.S. of my early years, in which I had determined
write myself out; as I was placed by Fortune
mong a class of men to whom my ideas would
have been nonsense — I had meant that the
book would have lain by me, in the fond hope
that, some time or other, even after I was no
more, ~~that~~ my thoughts would fall into the
hands of somebody capable of appreciating
their value. — It sets off thus ——————

Observations, hints, songs, scraps of Poetry &c. by
R. B. — a man who had little art in making
money, & still less in keeping it; but was, however,
man of some sense, a great deal of honesty, & unbounded
odwill to every creature, rational & irrational. — As
was but little indebted to scholastic education, &
ed at a plough-tail, his performances must
strongly tinctured with his unpolished, rustic
ay of life; but as I believe they are really his
wn, it may be some entertainment to a curious
observer

Observer of human-nature to see how a Ploughman
thinks & feels, under the pressure of love, ambition,
anxiety, grief, with the like cares & passions, which
however diversified by the <u>modes</u> & <u>manners</u> of
of life, operate pretty much alike; I believe, on
all the Species. ——————

"There are numbers in the world, who do not want
"sense, to make a figure; so much as an opinion of
"their own abilities, to put them upon recording their
"observations, & allowing them the same importance
"which they do to those which appear in print."——
                                        Shenstone.——

"Pleasing, when youth is long expired, to trace -
"The forms our pencil, or our pen designed!
"Such was our youthful air, & shape, & face,
• "Such the soft image of our youthful mind."-
                                        Ibidem ——

vid — 83] Notwithstanding all that has been said against love, respecting the folly & weakness it leads a young inexperienced mind into; still, I think it in a great measure deserves the highest encomiums that have been passed on it. — If any thing on earth deserves the name of rapture or transport, it is the feelings of green eighteen, in the company of the Mistress of his heart, when she repays him with an equal return of affection. —

9] There is certainly some connection between Love, Music, & Poetry; & therefore, I have always thought a fine touch of Nature, that passage in a modern love composition —

"As toward her cot he jogg'd along,
"Her name was frequent in his song"

For my own part, I never had the least thought, or inclination, of turning Poet till I got once heartily in love; & then Rhyme & Song were, in a manner, the spontaneous language of my heart. —

1] I entirely agree with that judicious Philosopher, Mr Smith, in his excellent Theory of Moral sentiments, that Remorse

is the most painful sentiment that can embitter the
human bosom. — Any ordinary pitch of fortitude may
bear up tolerably well under those calamities, in the
procurement of which, we ourselves have had no har[d]
but when our own follies, or crimes, have made us
miserable & wretched, to bear it up with manly firmn[ess]
& at the same time have a proper penitential sense o[f]
our misconduct — is a glorious effort of self-comm[and]

Of all the numerous ills that hurt our peace,
That press the soul, or wring the mind with anguis[h]
Beyond comparison the worst are those
That to our Folly, or our Guilt we owe. —
In ev'ry other circumstance, the mind
Has this to say — "It was no deed of mine"
But when to all the evil of misfortune
This sting is added — "Blame thy foolish Self!
Or worse far, the pangs of keen Remorse
The torturing, gnawing consciousness of guilt
Of guilt, perhaps, where we've involved others;
The young, the innocent, who fondly loved u[s]
Nay more, that very love their cause of ruin

'burning Hell! in all thy store of torments
There's not a keener lash! ——

Lives there a man so firm, who, while his heart
Feels all the bitter horrors of his crime,
Can reason down its agonising throbs;
And after proper purpose of amendment,
Can firmly force his jarring thoughts to peace?
O happy! happy! enviable man!
O, glorious magnamity of soul!

——————

March—84? Intended for a character in a tragedy I was
projecting —

"All devil as I am, a damned wretch,
A hardened, stubborn, unrepenting villain,
Still my heart melts at human wretchedness;
And with sincere, tho' unavailing, sighs
I view the helpless children of distress. —
With tears indignant, I behold th' Oppressor
Rejoicing in the honest man's destruction,
Whose unsubmitting heart was all his crime:—

Even you, ye hapless crew! I pity you,
Ye, whom the seeming good think sin to pity.
Ye

Ye poor, despised, abandoned vagabonds,
Whom Vice, as usual, has turned o'er to Ruin. –
O, but for kind, tho' ill-requited friends,
I had been driven forth like you, forlorn.
The most detested, worthless wretch among you

O, injured God! thy goodness has endowed me
With talents passing most of my compeers,
Which I in just proportion have abused,
As far surpassing other common villains,
As thou in nat'ral parts hast given me more!

I have often observed, in the course of my experience of human life, that every man, even the
worst, have something good about them; though
very often nothing else than a happy temperament
of constitution inclining them to this, or that
virtue. — For this reason, no man can say in what
degree any other person, besides himself, can be, with
strict justice, called <u>wicked</u>. — Let any of the stricter
character for regularity of conduct among us, examine
impartially how many vices he has never been guilty

not from any care or vigilance, but for want of op-
rtunity, or some accidental circumstance intervening;
w many of the weaknesses of mankind he has es-
ped, because he was out of the line of such tempt-
tion: & what often, if not always, weighs more
an all the rest; how much he is indebted to the
orld's good opinion, because the world does not know
ll; I say, any man who can thus think, will
an the failings, nay, the faults & crimes, of
ankind around him, with a brother's eye. —

ch-84?] I have often courted the acquaintance of that part
mankind, commonly known by the ordinary phrase
'Blackguards; sometimes farther than was
nsistent with the safety of my character: those
o by thoughtless prodigality, or headstrong passions,
ve been driven to ruin. — Though disgraced by
llies, nay sometimes "stained with guilt, & crimsoned
r with crimes," I have yet found among them, in
ot a few instances, some of the noblest virtues,
gnanimity, Generosity, disinterested Friendship, &
en Modesty, in the highest perfection. —

As I am what the men of the world, if they knew such a man, would call a whimsical mortal; I have various sources of pleasure & enjoyment which are, in a manner, peculiar to myself; or some here & there one other out-of-the-way person. — Such is the peculiar pleasure I take in the season of winter, more than the rest of the year — This, I believe, may be partly owing to my misfortunes giving my mind a melancholy cast; but there is Something even in the — "Mighty tempest, & the hoary waste

"Abrupt & deep, stretched o'er the buried earth" — which raises the mind to a serious sublimity, favorable to every thing great & noble —— There is scarcely any earthly object gives me more — I do not know if I should call it pleasure — but something which exalts me, something which enraptures me — than to walk in the sheltered side of a wood, or high plantation, in a cloudy winter day, & hear a stormy wind howling among the trees, & raving o'er the plain. — It is best season for devotion: my mind is rapt up in a kind of enthusiasm to HIM who, in the pompous language of the Hebrew Bard, "walks on the wings of the wind"

one of these seasons, just after a tract of misfortunes, I composed
the following — (Vide, the poem in my works, beginning-
"The wintry west extends his blast &c. &c.

Shenstone finely observes, that love-verses writ without
any real passion, are the most nauseous of all conceits; I
have often thought that no man can be a proper critic of
love-composition, except he himself, in one or more instances,
have been a warm votary of this passion. — As I have been
all along a miserable dupe to love, & have been led into a
thousand weaknesses & follies by it, for that reason I put
the more confidence in my critical skill in distinguishing
foppery & Conceit from Real Passion & Nature. — Whether
the following song will stand the test, I will not pretend
to say, because it is my own; only I can say it was,
at the time, real. —

(Vide my song — Nanie O)

I think the whole species of ~~mankind~~ young men may
rally enough
divided into two grand classes, which I shall call, the GRAVE,
the MERRY; though by the bye, these terms do not with propri-
enough express my ideas. — ~~The GRAVE~~, I shall cast
to the usual division, of those who are goaded on by ~~the~~
love

love of money, & those whose darling wish is to make a figure in the world. — The MERRY, are the Men of Pleasure, of all denominations; the jovial lads who have too much fire & spirit to have any settled rule of action but without much deliberation, follow the strong impulse of nature: the Thoughtless, the Careless, the Indolent; & in particular he, who with a happy sweetness of natural temper, & a chearful vacancy of thought, steals through life; generally indeed in poverty & obscurity, but poverty & obscurity are only evils to him who can sit gravely down & make a refining comparison between his own situation & that of others; & lastly, to grace the quorum, such are generally those whose heads are capable of all the tossings of Genius, & whose hearts are warmed with all the delicacy of Feeling. —

As the grand end of Human Life is to cultivate an intercourse with that BEING to whom we owe life, with every enjoyment that can render life delightful; & to maintain an integritive° conduct towards our fellow-creatures; that by forming Piety & Virtue into habit, we may be fit members for that society of the Pious & the Good, which reason & revelation teach us to expect beyond the grave —— I do not see that the turn of mind & pursuits of my son

poverty & obscurity [4¹] are in the least more inimical to
sacred interests of Piety & Virtue, than the, even lawful,
riding & straining after the world's riches & honors: & I
not see but that he may gain Heaven as well (which by the
e is no mean consideration) who steals through the vale
life, amusing himself with every little flower that
ture throws in his way; as he who straining straight
ward, & perhaps bespattering all about him, gains
one of life's little eminences, where, after all, he can,
nly see & be seen a little more conspicuously, than
that, in the pride of his heart, he is apt to term, the
oor, indolent devil he has left behind him. ——

————————————

here is a noble sublimity, a heart-melting tenderness in some of the
r ancient Ballads, which shew them to be the work of a masterly
nd; & it has often given me many a heart-ach, to reflect that
ch glorious old Bards — Bards, who very probably owed all
eir talents to native genius, yet have described the exploits of Heroes
pangs of disappointment, & the meltings of Love, with such
e strokes of nature; and — O! mortifying to a Bard's
nity! there very names are now "Buried 'mong the wreck
f things which were." ——

O ye illustrious Names unknown! who could feel so
ngly, & describe so well; the last, the meanest of the
                                        Muses'

Muses' strain — one who though far inferiour to your flight
yet eyes your path, & with trembling wing would sometimes
after you — a poor, rustic Bard unknown, pays this sym-
-pathetic pang to your memory. — Some of you tell us,
all the charms of verse, that you have been unfortunate
in the world — unfortunate in love: he, too, has felt
loss of his little fortune, the loss of friends, & worse than
all, the loss of the woman he adored. — Like you, all
consolation was his Muse: she taught him in rustic
measures to complain. — Happy, could he have done
with your strength of imagination, & flow of verse! —
May the turf lie lightly on your bones! And may
you now enjoy that solace & rest which this world rarely
gives to the heart tuned to all the feelings of Poesy & Love.

_____

This is all that, & perhaps more than, is worth
quoting, in my M. S. S. _____

To the Right Honble [43]the W__ P__ esquire ———

At the juncture of the king's illness, while the Regency bill was pending, & when every body expected the Premier's downfall, Addresses crouded in to him from all quarters; &, among the rest, the following appeared in a Newspaper. — The Addressers, the late Distillers of Scotland, had just been lately ruined by a positive breach of the Public faith, in a most partial tax laid on by the House of Commons, to favour a few opulent English Distillers, who, it seems, were of vast Electioneering consequence. ———

Sir

while fussy Burgesses croud your gate, sweating under the weight of heavy Addresses permit the quondam Distillers in that part of G—B—called S——, to approach you; not with venal approbation, but with fraternal condolence; not as what you just now are, & for some time have been, but what, in all probability, you will shortly be; — We will have the merit of not deserting our friends in the day of their calamity, & you will have the satisfaction of perusing at least one honest Address. —

You

You are well acquainted with the dissection of human
nature; nor do you need the assistance of a fellow-creat
bosom to inform you, that Man is always a selfish
often a perfidious being. — This assertion, howeve
the hasty conclusions of superficial observation ma
doubt of it, or the raw inexperience of youth ma
deny it, those who make the fatal experiment as
have done, will feel it. — You are a statesman,
consequently are not ignorant of the traffic of the
Corporation Compliments. — The little Great Ma
who drives the Borough to market, & the very Gr
Man who buys the Borough in that market, the
two, do the whole business; & you well know, they, like
-wise, have their price. — With that sullen disdain
which you can so well assume, rise, illustrious Si
& spurn these hireling efforts of venal stupidity
They are the compliments of a man's friends o
the morning of his execution: they take a decen
farewell, resign you to your fate, & hurry away
from your approaching hour. ———

. If Fame say true, & omens be not very much mistak
You are about to make your exit from that world where
the sun of gladness gilds the paths of prosperous me

permit us, great Sir, with the sympathy of fellow-feeling,
hail your passage to the realms of ruin. — Whether the
sentiment proceed from the selfishness or cowardice of mankind, is immaterial; but to a child of misfortune, pointing
him out those who are still more unhappy, is giving him
some degree of positive enjoyment — In this light, Sir, our
own fall may be again useful to you: though not
exactly in the same way, it is not perhaps the first
time it has gratified your feelings. — It is true, the
triumph of your evil star is exceedingly despiteful. — At
an age when others are the votaries of Pleasure, or underlings
in business, you had attained the highest wish of a
British Statesman; &, with the ordinary date of human
life, what a prospect was before you! — Deeply
rooted in Royal favor, you overshadowed the Land;
the birds of passage, which follow Ministerial sunshine through every clime of Political faith & manners,
flocked to your branches; & the beasts of the field,
the lordly possessors of hills & vallies, crouded under
our shade. — "But behold a watcher, a holy one
came down from Heaven, and cried aloud, & said thus,
Hew down the tree, & cut off his branches, shake off
his leaves, & scatter his fruit: let the beasts get away
from under it, & the fowls from his branches." — A blow
from

from an unthought of quarter, one of those terrible accidents which peculiarly mark the hand of Omnipotence, overs... your career, & laid all your fancied honors in the dust

But turn your eyes, Sir, to the tragic scenes of our fate. — An ancient Nation that for many ages had g... lantly maintained the unequal struggle for independance with her much more powerful neighbour, at last agrees a Union, which should ever after make them one People. — In consideration of certain circumstances, it was covenanted that the former should enjoy a stipula... alleviation in her share of the public burdens; particu... in that branch of the revenue called the Excise. — T... just privilege has of late given great umbrage to som... interested, powerful individuals of the more potent half the empire, & they have spared no wicked pains; un... insidious pretexts to subvert, what they yet dreaded t... spirit of their ancient enemies too much, openly to attack. — In this conspiracy we fell: nor did we alo... suffer; our Country was deeply wounded. — A nu... of, we will say it, respectable individuals, largely... ged in trade, where we were not only useful, but absolutely necessary to our Country in her dearest in... rests; we, with all that was near & dear to us, we... sacrificed

...crificed without remorse to the infernal deity of Political Expediency! At that sound policy, the good of the Whole; we fell to gratify the wishes. of dark Envy, & the views of unprincipled Ambition! Your foes, Sir, were avowed: you fell in the face of day: your enemies were too brave, to take an ungenerous advantage.— On the contrary, our enemies, to compleat our overthrow, contrived to make their guilt appear the villainy of a Nation.—— Your downfall only drags with you, your private friends & partisans; in our misery are, more or less, involved, the most numerous & the most valuable part of the Community; All those who immediately depend on the cultivation of the soil, from the landlord of a province down to his lowest hind.——

Allow us, Sir, yet farther, just to hint at another rich vein of comfort in the dreary regions of Adversity. the gratulations of an approving conscience. — In a certain Great Assembly of which you are a distinguished member, panegyrics on your private virtues have so often. wounded your delicacy, that we shall not distress you with any thing on the subject. — There is, however, one part of your public conduct which our feelings will not permit us to pass in silence; our gratitude must trespass on your modesty; we mean, worthy Sir, your whole behaviour to the Scots Distillers. — In evil hours, when obtrusive recollection pressed bitterly on the sense, it that, Sir, come like a healing angel, & speak the peace to your soul which the world can neither give nor take away!——

We the honor to be, Sir, your sympathising fellow-suffer, & grateful humble serv.ts

John Barleycorn, Præses——

To Miss M:murdo, daughter to John M:murdo Factor 1793
the Duke of Queensberry; inclosing a ballad I had com
sed on her. — The ballad will appear in Pleyel's Pub-
cation of Scots Songs; & begins—
⁀There was a lass & she was fair ———

Madam

amid the profusion of complimentary add
which your age, sex & accomplishments will now bring y
permit me to approach with my devoirs, which, howeve
deficient may be their consequence in other respects, ha
the double novelty & merit, in these frivolous, hollow tim
of being poetic & sincere. — In the inclosed ballad, I ha
I think, hit off a few outlines of your portrait. — Th
personal charms, the purity of mind, the ingenuous
naïveté of heart & manners, in my heroine, are, I
flatter myself, a pretty just likeness of Miss M:mur
in a Cottager. — Every composition of this kind m
have a series of Dramatic incident in it; so I have
recourse to my invention, to finish the rest of my
ballad. ————
So much from the Poet: now, let me add a
wishes which every man, who has himself the hon
of being a father, must breathe, when he sees Fem
Youth, Beauty & Innocence about to enter into t
mu

uch chequered & very precarious world. — May you, my my Madam, escape that Frivolity, which threatens universally to vade the minds & manners of Fashionable Life — To pass by rougher, & still more degenerate sex, the mob of fashionable male youth, what are they? — Are they any thing? — They rattle, laugh, sing, dance, finger a lesson, or perhaps turn over he pages of a fashionable Novel; but are their minds sto. d with any information, worthy of the noble powers of ason & judgement; or do their hearts glow with sentiment, dent, generous & humane? — Were I to poetise on the bject, I would call them, the butterflies of the human kind: markable only for, & distinguished only by, the idle variety their gaudy glare; sillily straying from one blossoming eed to another, without a meaning, & without an aim; the ot prey of every pirate of the skies, who thinks them worth s while as he wings his way by them; & speedily by ntry time, swept to that oblivion whence they might as ll never have appeared. —————

Amid this croud of Nothings, may you, Madam, be mething! — May you be a Character, dignified as Rati. al & Immortal Being! — A still ~~more formidable~~

A still more formidable plague in life, unfeeling, rested Selfishness, is a contagion too impure to touch . — The selfish drift to bless yourself alone; to build your ne on another's ruin; to look on the child of Misfortune hout commiseration, or even the victim of Folly without Pity —

Pity——— these, & every other feature of a heart rotten at the core, are what you are totally incapable of. ———

These wishes, Madam, are of no consequence to You but to Me, they are of the utmost; as they give me an opportunity of declaring with what respect I have the honor to be,

&c &c. ———

To the Earl of Glencairn (51)   **20**   1787

My Lord,   I wanted to purchase a profile of your Lordship
which I was told was to be got in town; but I am truly
sorry to see that a blundering Painter has spoilt a "human
face divine." — The inclosed stanzas I intended to have written
on a picture, or profile, shade of your Lordship, could I have been
so happy as to procure one with any thing of a likeness. —
as I will soon return to my shades, I wanted to have something
like a material object for my gratitude; I wanted to have
it in my power to say to a friend, There is my noble
Patron, my generous Benefactor. — Allow me, my Lord, to
offer my warm, ~~my fond~~ request, to be permitted to
publish these verses. — I conjure your Lordship, by
the honest throe of gratitude, by the generous wish of
benevolence, by all the powers & feelings which compose
the magnanimous mind, do not deny me this my
darling petition — I owe much, very much indeed,
to your Lordship; &, what has not in some other
instances been always the case with me, the weight
of the obligation is a pleasing load. — I trust I
have a heart as independant as your Lordship's, than
which I can say nothing more; & I would not be beholden
to favours which would crucify my feelings. — Your
                                              dignified

dignified character in life, & manner of supporting that character, are flattering to my ~~British~~ pride; I would be jealous of the fluidity of my grateful attachment, where I was under the patronage of a of the much-favored sons of Fortune. — Almost every Poet has celebrated his Patrons, particularly wh they were names dear to Fame, & illustrious in their country; allow me then, my Lord, if you think the verses have intrinsic merit, to tell th world how much I have the honor to be,

Your Lordship's highly indebted
& ever grateful, humble serv.t

To Crawford Tait Esq: Jun.r of Parkplace —— 1·78—

Dear Sir

Allow me to introduce to your acquaintance the bearer, Mr Will.m Duncan, a friend of mine whom I have long known & long loved. — His father, whose only son he is, has a decent little Property in Ayrshire, & has bred the young man to the Law; in which department he comes up an adventurer to your Good Town. — I shall give you my friend's character in two words: as to his head, he has talents enough & more than enough for common life; as to his heart, when Nature had kneaded the kindly clay that composes it, she said, "I can no more." ——

You, my good Sir, were born under kinder stars; but your fraternal sympathy, I well know, can enter fully into the feelings of the young man who enters life with the laudable ambition to do something & to be something among his fellow creatures; but whom the consciousness of friendless obscurity presses to the earth & wounds to the soul. — Even the fairest of his virtues are against him. — That independant spirit & that ingenuous modesty, qualities inseparable from a noble mind, are, with the Million, circumstances not a

little

little disqualifying. — That pleasure is in the power of the Fortunate & the Happy, to glad the heart of such depress Youth, by their notice & patronage! — I am not angry with mankind at their deaf economy of the purse. — The goods of this world cannot be divided without being lessened. — But why be a niggard of that which bestows bliss on a fellow-creature, yet takes nothing from their own means of enjoyment? — We wrap ourselves up in the cloak of our own better fortune, & turn away our eyes, lest the wants & woes of our brother-mortals should disturb the selfish apathy of our souls. —

I am the worst hand in the world at asking a favor. — That indirect address, that insinuating implication, which without any positive request, plainly expresses your wish, is not a ~~quality~~ talent to be acquired at a plough-tail. — Tell me, for you can, in what periphrasis of language, in what circumvolution of phrase, I shall envelope yet not conceal this plain story — "My "dear Mr Tait, my friend Mr Duncan whom I have "the pleasure of introducing to you, is a young man "lad of your own profession, & a gentleman of much "modesty & great worth. — Perhaps it may be in your power

(55).

assist him in the, to him, important consideration of getting a Place; but at all events, your notice & acquaintance will be him a very great acquisition; & I dare pledge myself that he will never disgrace your favor."—

You may probably be surprised, Sir, at such a letter from me: 'tis, I own, in the usual way of calculating these matters, more than our acquaintance entitles me to. — But my answer is short; of all the men at our time of life whom I knew in Edin:, you are most accessible on the side on which I have assailed you. — You are very much altered indeed from what you were when I knew you, if Generosity point the path you will not tread, or Humanity call to you in vain. ——

I am &c. &c —

To Miss H— C— (56)   1789 or 90

Madam,

some rather unlooked for accidents have prevented me from doing myself the honor of a second visit to A————, as I was so hospitably invited, & so positively meant to have done. — However I still hope to have that pleasure before the busy mo of harvest begin. —

I inclose you two of my late pieces as some kind of ~~compensation~~ return for the pleasure I have received in perusing a certain M.S.S. volume of Poems in the possession of Capt. R————. To repay one with "an old song," is a proverb who. force you, Madam, I know will not allow. — Wha is ~~true~~ said of illustrious descent is I believe equally true of a talent for Poesy; none ever despised it who had pretensions to it. — It is often a tra of thought of mine, when I am disposed to be melancholly, the fates && characters of the rhy tribe. — There is not, among all the martyrolog
ever

...enned, so rueful a narrative as the lives of the Poets.—
...n the comparative view of wretches, the criterion is not,
...what they are doomed to suffer, but how they are
...formed to bear —— Take a being of our kind, give him a
...stronger imagination & a more delicate sensibility (which
...etween them will ever engender a more ungovernable set
...f passions) than are the usual lot of man; implant
...n him an irresistible impulse to some idle vagary, such
...s arranging wild-flowers in fantastical nosegays,
...acing the grasshopper to his haunt by his chirping song,
...atching the frisks of the little minnows in the sunny
...ool, or hunting after the intrigues of wanton butterflies;
...n short, send him adrift after some pursuit which
...all eternally mislead him from the paths of lucre, &
...t curse him with a keener relish than any man
...ving for the pleasures that lucre can purchase; lastly,
...ll up the measure of his woes by bestowing on
...im a spurning sense of his own dignity; & you
...ave created a wight nearly as miserable as a Poet. —
...To you, Madam, I need not recount the fairy pleasures
...e Muse bestows to counterbalance this catalogue of evils.
...Bewitching Poesy is like bewitching Woman; she has in
...ll ages been accused of misleading mankind from the
counsels

counsels of Wisdom & the paths of Prudence, involving them in difficulties, baiting them with Poverty, branding them with Infamy, & plunging them in the whirling vortex of Ruin; yet, where is the man but must own that all our happiness on earth is not worthy the name, that even the holy hermit's solitary prospect of paradisical bliss is but the glitter of a northern sun rising over a frozen region, compared with the many pleasures the nameless raptures that we owe to the lovely queens of the heart of Man! —

in the year 17 93, when Royalist & Jacobin had set all Britain. by
e ears, because I unguardedly, rather under the temptation of
ing witty than disaffected, had declared my sentiments in
vor of Parliamentary Reform, in the manner of that
me. I was accused to the Board of Excise of being a
Republican, & was very near being turned adrift in the
ide world on that account. — Mr Erskine of Mar, a
gentleman indeed, wrote to my friend Glenriddell to know
f I was really out of place on account of my political
principles; & if so, he proposed a subscription among the
friends of Liberty for me, which he offered to head, that
might be no pecuniary loser by my political integrity. —
This was the more generous, as I had not the honor of
ing known to Mr Erskine. I wrote him as
ollows. —

Sir,

degenerate as Human Nature is said to be, & in many
stances, worthless & unprincipled it certainly is, still there are
ght examples to the contrary; examples, that even in the
e of superiour Beings must shed a lustre on the name of
an: — Such an example have I now before me, when
u, Sir, came forward to patronise & befriend a distant,
obscure

obscure stranger; merely because Poverty had made him helpless, & his British hardihood of mind had provoked the arbitrary wantonness of Power. — My much esteemed friend, Mr Riddell of Glenriddell, has just read me a paragraph of a letter he had from you. — Accept, Sir, of the silent throb of gratitude; for words would but mock the emotions of my soul. —

You have been misinformed, as to my final dismission from the Excise: I still am in the service. — Indeed, but for the exertions of a gentleman who must be known to you, Mr Graham of Fintry, a gentleman who has ever been my warm & generous friend, I had, without so much as a hearing, or the smallest previous intimation, been turned adrift, with my helpless family, to all the horrors of Want. Had I had any other resource, probably I might have saved them the trouble of a dismissal; but the little money I gained by my Publication, is almost every guinea embarked, to save from ruin an only brother; who, though one of the worthiest, is by no means one of the most fortunate of men.

In my defence to their accusations, I said, that whatever might be my sentiments of Republics, ancient or modern, to Britain, I abjured the idea. — That a Constitution which

its original principles, experience had proved to be every way
...ted for our happiness in society, it would be insanity to an...
...tried visionary theory. — That, in consideration of my being
...ated in a department, however humble, immediately in the hands
...the people in power, I had forborne taking any active part,
...ther personally, or as an author, in the present business of
...eform. — But that, where I must declare my sentiments,
...ould say that there existed a system of corruption between
...Executive Power & the Representative part of the Legislature,
...ich boded no good to our glorious Constitution; & which every
...triotic Briton must wish to see amended. — Some such
...timents as these I stated in a letter to my generous Patron,
...Graham, which he laid before the Board at large, where
...seems my last remark gave great offence; & one of our
...pervisors general, a Mr Corbet, was instructed to enquire,
...the spot, into my conduct, & to document me — "that my
...siness was to act, not to think; & that whatever might
...Men or Measures, it was my business to be silent &
...edient". — Mr Corbet was likewise my steady friend; so,
...tween Mr Graham & him, I have been partly forgiven.
...ly, I understand that all hopes of my getting officially
...ward are blasted. ——————

Now, Sir, to the business in which I would more
...mediately interest you. — The partiality of my Countrymen
has

has brought me forward as a man of genius, & has given me
a Character to support. — In the Poet, I have avowed manly &
independant sentiments, which I trust will be found in the
Man. — Reasons of no less weight than the support of a
wife & children have pointed out as the eligible, & indeed the
only eligible line of life for me, my present occupation. —
Still, my honest fame is my dearest concern; & a thousand
times have I trembled at the idea of the degrading epithets that
Malice, or Misrepresentation may affix to my name. —
I have often, in blasting anticipation, listened to some
future hackney, Magazine scribbler, with the heavy malice of
savage stupidity, exulting in his hireling paragraphs
that "Burns, notwithstanding the fanfaronade of inde-
"pendance to be found in his works, & after having
"held forth to Public View & Public Estimation as a man
"some genius, yet, quite destitute of resources within himself
"to support this borrowed dignity, he dwindled into a paltry
"Exciseman; & slunk out the rest of his insignificant
"existence in the meanest of pursuits & among the vilest
"of mankind." ——————

In your illustrious hands, Sir, permit me to lodge

y strong disavowal (63) & defiance of these slanderous falsehoods.— BURNS was a poor man, from birth; & an Exciseman, by necessity: but—I will say it!—the sterling of his honest worth, no poverty could debase; & his independant British mind, Oppression might bend, but could not subdue!— Have not I, to me, a more precious stake in my Country's welfare, than the richest Dukedom in it?— I have a large family of children, & the probability of more.—I have three sons, whom, I see already, have brought with them into the world souls ill qualified to inhabit the bodies of slaves.— Can I look tamely on, & see any machination to wrest from them, the birthright of my boys, the little independant Britons in whose veins runs my own blood?— No! I will not!—should my heart stream around my attempt to defend it!—

        Does any man tell me, that my feeble efforts can be of no service; & that it does not belong to my humble station to meddle with the concerns of a People?—I tell him, that it is on such individuals as I, that for the hand of support & the eye of intelligence, a Nation has to rest.— The uninformed mob may swell a nation's bulk, & the titled, tinsel Courtly throng may be its feathered ornament, but the number of those who are

are elevated enough in life, to reason & reflect; & yet low enough to keep clear of the venal contagion of a Court; these are a Nation's strength. —

One small request more: when you have honored this letter with a perusal, please commit it to the flames BURNS, in whose behalf you have so generously interested yourself, I have here, in his native colours, drawn as he is; but should any of the people in whose hands is the very bread he eats, get the least knowledge of the picture, it would ruin the poor Bard for ever.—

My Poems having just come out in another edition, I beg leave to present you with a copy; as a small mark of that high esteem & ardent gratitude with which I have the honor to be —

&c. —

To Alex.^r Cunningham Writer in Edin.^r, some little time after his marriage; & after, through his recommendation that I had been presented with a Diploma from the Edin. Company of Royal Archers ——————

133

No! I will not attempt an apology. — Amid all my hurry of business — grinding the faces of the Publican & Sinner on the merciless wheels of the Excise; making ballads, & then singing them ~~over~~ to my drink; over & above all, the correcting the Press-work of two different Publications; — still, still I might have stolen five minutes to dedicate to one of the first of my Friends & Fellow-creatures. —————— I might have done as I do at present, snatched an hour near "witching time of night," & scrawled a page or two. — I might have congratulated my friend on his marriage; or, I might have thanked the Caledonian Archers for the honor they have done me: though, to do myself justice, I intended to have done both in rhyme, else had done both before now. ——

Well, then! here is your good health! for I have set a
nipperkin of toddy by me, by way of spell to keep away
the meikle horned Deil, or any of his subaltern Imps who
may be on their nightly rounds. ——

But what shall I write to you? — "The voice said, cry! —
said, what shall I cry!" — O thou Spirit! whatever
thou art, or wherever thou makest thyself visible! — Be
thou a Bogle by the eerie side of an auld thorn, in the dreary
glen, through which the herd-callen maun bicker in his
gamin route frae the fauld — Be thou a Brownie,
set, in the dead of night, to thy task by the blazing ingle; or
in the solitary barn, where the repercussions of thy iron
flail half-affrights thyself, as thou performest the work of
twenty of the sons of men, ere the cock-crowing summon
thee to thy ample cogue of substantial brose — Be thou a
Kelpie, haunting the ford, or ferry, in the starless night,
mixing thy laughing yell with the howling of the storm,
& the roaring of the flood, as thou viewest the perils and
miseries of man, on the foundering horse, or in the
trembling boat — ! — Or, lastly, be thou a Ghost, paying
nocturnal visits to the hoary ruins of decayed grandeur;
performing thy mystic rites in the shadow of the time-worn
church

church, while the moon looks, without a cloud, on the silent ghastly dwellings of the Dead beside thee; or taking thy stand by the bedside of the Villain, or the Murderer, pourtraying on their dreaming fancy, pictures, dreadful as the horrors of unveiled Hell, & terrible as the wrath of incensed Deity—— Come! thou Spirit! but not in these horrid forms; come, with the milder, gentle, easy inspirations which thou breathest around the wig of a prating Advocate, or the tête of a tea-drinking Gossip, while their tongues run at the light-horse gallop of clishmaclaver for ever & ever—— Come, & assist a poor devil who is quite jaded in the attempt to share half an idea among half a hundred words; to fill up four quarto pages; while he has not gotten one single sentence of recollection, information, or remark, worth recording.——

    I feel, I feel the presence of supernatural assistance! Circled in the embrace of my elbow-chair, my breast labors like the bloated Sybil on her three-footed stool, like her too, labors with nonsense.— Nonsense! Auspicious Name!!! Tutor, Friend & Finger-post, the mystic mazes of Law; the cadaverous paws of Physic; and particularly in the sightless soaring avings of School-Divinity who, leaving Common Sense confounded at his strength of pinion, Reason delirious with eyeing his giddy flights, & Truth creeping back into the bottom of her well, cursing the hour in which she offered her scorned alliance to the Wizard Power of Theologic Vision——— raves abroad on all the winds,—. In Earth, discord! A gloomy Heaven above, opening her jealous gates to the nineteen thousandth part of the tithe of mankind! And below, an inescapable & reprovable Hell, expanding its levathan jaws for the vast residue of mortals!.;!"——— O, Doctrine! comfortable & healing to the weary, wounded soul of man!— Ye sons & daughters of Affliction, ye sauvres Miserables, to whom day brings no pleasure, night yields no rest, be comforted!— Tis but re, to nineteen hundred thousand, that your situation ill mend in this world; & 'tis nineteen hundred thousand, to one, that you will be damned, eternally, the world to come!———

But of all nonsense, religious nonsense is the st nonsensical, so enough, & more than enough of it.— ly, by the bye, will you, or can you tell me, my dear unningham,, why a religioso turn of mind has always

a

a tendency to narrow, & illiberalize the. the heart? – or are orderly; they may be just; nay, I have known them merciful: but still your children of ~~super-sancti~~ super-sanctity move among their fellow-creatures with a nostril snuffing putrescence, & a foot spurning filth, – in short, with that conceited dignity which your titled Douglases, Hamiltons, Gordons, or any other of your Scots Lordlings of seven centuries standing, display when they accidentally mix among the many-aproned sons of Mechanical life. – I remember, in my plough-boy days I could not conceive it possible that a noble Lord could be a Fool, or that a Godly man could be a Knave. – How ignorant are plough-boys! – Nay, I have since discovered that a Godly Woman may be a ——— ! ——— But hold – this Rum is generous Antigua; so, a very unfit menstruum for scandal.

Apropos, how do you like, I mean really like, the Marriage life? – Ah, my Friend! Matrimony is quite a different thing from what your love-sick youth & sighing girls take it to be! – But marriage, we are told, is appointed by G——, & I shall never quarrel with

ith any of His institutions. — I am a Husband of older
inding than you, & I shall give you my ideas of the
appiness of the Conjugal State. — (En passant, you know
am no Latin, is not "conjugal" derived from "Jugum" a
oke!) — Well then, the scale of Good-wife-ship I divide
nto ten parts. — Goodnature, four; Goodsense, two; Wit,
ne; Personal Charms, viz. a sweet face, eloquent eyes,
ine limbs, graceful carriage, (I would add a fine waist too,
ut that is so soon spoilt you know) all these, One: as
for the other qualities belonging to, or attending on, a wife,
such as fortune, connections, education, (I mean, more than
the ordinary run) family-blood, &c. divide the two
emaining degrees among them as you please, only
emember that all these minor properties must be
xpressed by fractions; for there is not any one of
hem, in my aforesaid Scale, entitled to the dignity of
n Integer. ————

—

s for the rest of my fancies & reveries — How I
t lately with Miss Lesley Baillie, the most beautiful,
gant woman in the world — How I accompanied her
and —

and 'her Father's family fifteen [72] miles on their road, purer'd
to admire the loveliness of the works of God in such
unequalled display of them — Now, as I gallofed her
at night, I made a Ballad on her, of which the two follow-
stanzas are a part —

"Thou, bonie Lesley, art a Queen,
  Thy subjects we, before thee:
Thou, bonie Lesley, art divine,
  The hearts of men adore thee. —

The very Deil he could na skaith
  Whatever wad belang thee;
He'd look into thy bonie face,
  And say, "I canna wrang thee. —

Behold, all these are written in the chronicles of
my imaginations, & shall be read by thee, my dear
O Friend, & by thy beloved Spouse, my other dear
O Friend, at a more convenient season. —

Now, to thee, & to thy said bosom-companion,
be given, the precious things brought forth by the sun
& the precious things brought forth by the Moon;
the benignest influences of the Stars, & the living stre[am]
which flow from the fountains of life, & by the tree of
life, for ever & ever!

To Mr Corbet, Supervisor general of Excise ———

Sir,
I have in my time taken up the pen on several ticklish subjects, but none that ever cost me half so much as the language of supplication. — To open one's wants & woes to the mercy of another's benevolence, is a business so prostituted by the worthless & unfeeling, that a man of Principle & Delicacy shrinks from it as from Contamination. —

Mr S. — tells me that you wish to know from myself what are my views in desiring to change my situation Excise Division. — With the wish natural to man, of bettering his present situation, I have turned my thoughts towards the practibility of getting into a Port Division. — As I know that the General Super.rs are omnipotent in these matters, my honored friend, Mrs Dunlop of Dunlop, offered me to interest you in my behalf. — She told me that she was well acquainted with Mrs Corbet's goodness, & that on the score of former intimacy, she thought she could promise some influence with her: and added, with her

her usual sagacity & knowledge of human nature, that
the surest road to the good offices of a man was through
the mediation of the woman he loved. — On this
footing, Sir, I venture my application; else, not even
the known generosity of your character would have
emboldened me to address you thus. —

I have the honor &c.

To Mr Moodie — One of the ministers of Edin.r — 1792

Rev.d & Dear Sir —

  This will be presented you by a particular friend of mine, a Mr Clarke, Schoolmaster in Moffat, who has lately become the unfortunate & undeserved subject of persecution from some of his Employers. — The ostensible & assigned reason on their part is, some instances of severity to the boys under his care; but I have had the best opportunities of knowing the merits of the cause, & I assure you, Sir, that he is falling a sacrifice to the weakness of the MANY following in the cry of the Villainy of the FEW. — The business will now come before the Patrons of the School, who are, the Ministers, Magistrates & Town-council of Edin.r, & in that view I would interest your goodness in his behalf. — 'Tis true, Sir, & I feel the full force of the observation, that a man in my powerless, humble station very much mistakes himself, & very much mistakes the way of the world, when he dares presume to offer influence among so highly respectable a Body as the Patronage as I have mentioned; but what could I do?

a

A man of Abilities, a man of Genius, a man of Worth
and my Friend, before I would stand quietly & silent by
& see him perish thus, I would down on my knees to the
rocks & the mountains, & implore them to fall on his
Persecutors & crush their malice & them in deserved
destruction! — Believe me, Sir, he is a greatly
injured man. — The humblest individual, though, Alas!
he cannot to redress the wrong, may yet as ably attest
the fact, as a Lord. —— M.r Moodie's goodness I
well know; & that acquaintance with him I have the
honor to boast of, will forgive my addressing him thus
in favour of a Gentleman, whom, if he knew as
well, he would esteem as I do. ——

To Alexr Cunningham —   118.

Let me interest you, my dear Cunningham, in behalf of the
Gentleman who gives you this — He is a Mr Clarke of.
Moffat, principal schoolmaster there, & is at present suffering
severely under the persecution of one or two malicious but
powerful individuals of his employers. — He is accused of
harshness to some perverse dunces that were placed under
his care. — God help the Teacher, a man of genius &
sensibility, for such is my friend Clarke, when the blockhead Father presents him his booby son, & insists on
having the rays of science lighted up in a fellow's
head, whose scull is impervious & inaccessible by any
other way than a positive fracture with a cudgel! !
A fellow, whom in fact it savours of Impiety to attempt
making a scholar of, as he has been marked, a
"Blockhead", in the book of fate at the Almighty fiat of
his Creator. ——————————

The Patrons of Moffat-school are, the Ministers,
Magistrates & Town-Council of Edinr., & as the business
comes now before them, let me beg my dearest Friend
to do every thing in his power to serve the interests
of

of a man of genius, a man of worth, & a man whom I particularly respect & esteem — You know some good fellows among the Magistrates & Council, though, God knows, 'tis generally a very unfit soil for good fellows to flourish in, but particularly you have much to say with a Revd. Gentleman to whom you have the honor of being very nearly related; & whom this Country & Age have had the honor to produce — I need not name the Historian of Charles the fifth: — I tell him through the medium of his nephew's influence, that Mr. Clarke is a gentleman who will not disgrace even his Patronisation. —

I know the merits of the cause thouroughly; & I say it, that my friend is falling a sacrifice to prejudiced Ignorance, & envious, causeless Malice — God help the children of Dependance! Hated & persecuted by their enemies, & too often — Alas, almost unexceptionably, always — received by their friends with insulting disrespect, & heart-stinging reproach, under the thin disguises of cold civility, & humiliating advice —

O, to be a sturdy Savage, stalking in the pride of his independance amid the solitary wilds of his desarts! Rather than in civilized life helplessly to tremble for a subsistence

subsistence, precarious as the caprice of a fellow-creature!

Every man has his virtues, & no man is without his ~~other~~ failings; & curse on that privileged plaindealing of friendship, which, in the hour of my calamity, cannot reach forth the helping hand, without at the same time pointing out those failings, & assigning their share in my present distress. — My friends, (for such the world calls you, & such ye think yourselves to be,) pass by my Virtues if you please; but do, also, spare my follies: the first will witness in my breast for themselves, & the last will give pain enough to the ingenuous mind without you. — And since deviating, more, or less, from the paths of Propriety & Rectitude must be incident to Human-nature, do thou, Fortune, put it in my power, always from my own pocket to pay the penalties of those errors. — I do not want to be independant, that I may sin; but I want to be independant in my sinning. —

To return in this rambling letter to the subject I set out with, let me recommend my friend, Clarke, to your acquaintance & good offices: his Worth entitles him to the first, & his Gratitude will merit the last. —

1792

The following letter [80] which was sent by Mr Clarke to the Provost of "Odin", was of my writing

My Lord

It may be deemed presumption in a man, obscure & unknown as I am, & an entire stranger to your Lordship, to trouble you in this manner; but when I inform you that the subject on which I address you is of the last importance to me, & is so far connected with you, that on your determination, in a great measure, my fate must depend, I rely on your Lordship's goodness that you will think any farther apology unnecessary. — I have been for nearly five years schoolmaster in Moffat; an appointment of which, your Lordship will know, you, with the rest of the Magistracy & Town Council, together with the Clergy of "Odin", have the Patronage. — The trust with which these my highly respectable Patrons had honored me I have endeavoured to discharge with the utmost fidelity, & I hope, with a good degree of success: but of late, one or two powerful individuals of my employers ha[ve]

been

...n pleased to attack my reputation as a Teacher; have threaten'd
...less than to expell me the school; & are taking every method,
some of them, I will say it, insidious & unfair to the last
degree, to put their threats in execution.—The fault of
which I am accused is, some instances of severity to the
children under my care.—Were I to tell your Lordship,
that I am innocent of the charge; that any shade of cruelty,
chiefly that very black one of cruelty to tender infancy, will be allowed by every unbiassed
person who knows any thing of me, to be tints unknown
in my disposition; you would certainly & justly look on
all this <u>from me</u>, as words of course; so I shall trouble
you with nothing on the merits of my cause, untill I
have a fair hearing before my Rt. Honble Patrons.—
A fair hearing, my Lord, is what above all things I want;
& what I greatly fear, will be attempted to be denied
me.—It is to be insinuated, that I have vacated
my place; that I never was legally appointed; with
I know not how many pretences more, to hinder
the business from coming properly before your Lordship
& the other Patrons of the school: all which I deny;
& will insist on holding my appointment untill the
dignified Characters who gave it me, shall find
me unworthy of it—In your Lordship's great

acquaintance

acquaintance with Human-life, [52] you must have known of, & seen, many instances of Innocence, nay, of Merit disguised & obscured, & sometimes for ever buried, by the dark machinations of unprincipled Malevolence, & envious Craft; & till the contrary be made appear, 'tis at least equally probable that my case is in that unfortunate & undeserved predicament. —

I have the honor to be, &c.

To Mr. Smellie, introducing Mrs Riddel of Woodleypark to him ——

N°9

I sit down, my dear Sir, to introduce a young lady to you, & a lady in the first ranks of fashion too. — What a task! You, who care no more for the herd of animals called, "Young Ladies," than for the herd of animals called — "Young Gentlemen"; You, who despise & detest the groupings & combinations of Fashion — an idiot Painter! who seems industrious to place staring Fools, and unprincipled Knaves in the fore-ground of his Picture, while Men of Sense & Honesty are too often thrown into the dimmest shades. — Mrs Riddel who takes this letter to town with her, is a Character that even in your own way as a Naturalist & a Philosopher, would be an acquisition to your acquaintance. — The Lady too, is a votary of the Muses; and as I think I am somewhat of a judge in my own trade, I assure you that her verses, always correct, & often elegant, are very much beyond the common run of the Lady Poetesses of the day. — She is a great admirer of your Book; & hearing me say that I was acquainted with you, she begged to be known to you, as she is just going to pay her first visit to our Caledonian

Caledonian Capital.[84] — I told her that her best way was, to desire your intimate friend & her near relation Craigdarroch, to have you at his house while she was there; & lest you should think of a lively West-Indian girl of eighteen, as girls of eighteen too often deserve to be thought of, I should take care to remove that prejudice. To be impartial however, the Lady has one unlucky failing; a failing which you will easily discover, as she seems rather pleased with indulging it; & a failing which you will as easily pardon, as it is a sin that very much besets yourself: — where she dislikes, or despises, she is apt to make no more a secret of it — than where she esteems & respects. —

I will not send you the unmeaning "Compl.ts of the season" but I will send you, my warmest wishes, & most ardent prayers, that Fortune may never throw your subsistence on the mercy of a Knave, nor set your character on the judgement of a Fool! But that, upright & erect, you may walk to an honest grave, where men of letters shall say, here lies a man who did honor to Science; & men of worth shall say, here lies a man who did honor to Human Nature.—

thanks to Mr. Corbert for granting the request of page 73

Sir

When I was honored with your most obliging letter, I said to myself—"A simple letter of thanks will be a very poor return for so much kindness; I shall likewise send the gentleman a cargo of my best & newest rhymes."— However, my new Division holds me so very busy, & several things in it being rather new to me, my time has hitherto been totally engrossed.——When a man is strongly imprefsed with a sense of something he ought to do; at the same that want of leisure, or want of opportunity, or want of afsistance, or want of information, or want of paper, pen & ink, or any other of the many wants which Flesh is heir to—— When sense of Duty pulls one way, & Necefsity (or, Alas! too often Indolence under Necefsity's garb) pulls another; you are too well acquainted with poor Human Nature, to be told what a devil of a life that arch-vixen, Conscience, leads us.—— Old as I am in acquaintance, & growing grey in connection, with Slips, Frips, Failings, Frailties, Back slidings in the paths of grace, & Forward fa's upon
a

a naked wame, and all the other light-horse militia of Iniquity, never did my poor back suffer such scarification from the scourge of Conscience, as during these three weeks that your kind epistle has lain by me unanswered. — A negro wench under the rod of a West-Indian Mistress; a nurse under the caprice of a spoilt child, the only son & heir of a booby Squire; nay, a hen-peckt Husband under the displeasure of his virago Wife — were enviable predicaments to mine. — last, by way of compromise, I return you by this my most grateful thanks for all the generous friendship & disinterested patronage, for which, now & formerly, I have the honor to be indebted to you; and as to the Rhymes, another edition, in two volumes, of my Poems being in the Press, I shall beg leave to present a copy to Mrs Corbet, as my first, & I will venture to add, most effectual mediator with you on my behalf. —

I have the honor to be, &c.

A letter for Mr Clarke (see pages 75, 77, & 80) to send to Mr
Williamson, Factotum & Favorite to the Earl of Hopetoun —

Sir

      most sincerely do I regret that concurrence of accident,
prejudice & mistake, which, most unfortunately for me, has
subjected me, as master of Moffat Grammar-School, to the
displeasure of the Earl of Hopetoun & those in whom he placed
confidence. — Protestations of my innocence will, from
me, be thought words of course. — But I hope, & I
think I have some well-grounded reasons for that hope,
that the gentlemen in whose hands I immediately
am, the Right Honble Patrons of the School, will find the
charges against me groundless, & my claims just; & will
not allow me to fall a sacrifice to the insidious designs
of some, & the well-meant, though mis-informed, zeal of
others. — However, as disputes & litigations must be of
great hurt both to the School & Me, I most ardently
wish that it would suggest itself to Mr Williamson's good
sense & wish for the welfare of the country, the propriety
of dropping all disputes, & allowing me peaceable
admission to my school & the exercise of my function. —

                                 This

This, Sir, I am persuaded, will be serving all parties; will lay <u>me</u> under particular & lasting obligations to your goodness. — I propose opening school tomorrow; & the quiet possession of my schoolhouse is what I have to request of you; a request which if refused, I must be under the very disagreeable necessity of asking in the way pointed out by the laws of my Country. — Whatever you, Sir, may think of other parts of my conduct, you will at least grant the propriety of a man's straining every nerve in a contest, where not only Ruin but Infamy must attend his defeat. —

Bravo! Clarke. — In spite of Hopeton & his myrmidons thou camest off victorious! —————

To the Duke of Queensberry, — with, the Whistle. —

My Lord Duke

will you Grace pardon this approach
a poor Poet, who perhaps intruded on your converse
ith Princes to present you — all he has to offer — his
st Ballad; & to beg of you — all he has to ask — your
racious acceptance of it. — Whatever might ~~have~~ be my
inion of the merits of the poem, I would not have
ared to take the liberty of presenting it thus, but for your
Grace's acquaintance with the Dramatis Personæ of the
Piece —

When I first thought of sending my poem to your
Grace, I had some misgivings of heart about it. — Something
within me seemed to say — "A nobleman of the first rank
& the first taste, & who has lived in the first court of
Europe, what will he care for either you or your
Ballad? — Depend upon it that he will look on
"this business as some one or other of the many modifi-
"cations of that servility of soul, with which Authors, &
"particularly you, Poets, have ever approached the Great." —
No! said I to myself: I am conscious of the purity

of my motives. (9°) ─ And as I never crouch to any man but the man I have wronged; nor even him except he forgives me; I will approach his Grace with tolerable upright confidence, that were I & my Ballad poorer stuff than we are, the Duke of Queensberry's polite affability would make me welcome: as my sole motive is to shew how sincerely I have the honor to be,

My Lord Duke,

Your Grace's most devoted humble serv.

This was written shortly after I had the honor of being introduced to the Duke, at which introduction I spent the evening with him, when he treated me with the most distinguished politeness, & marked attention. — Though I am afraid his Grace's character as a Man of worth is very equivocal, yet he certainly is a Nobleman of the first taste, & a Gentleman of the first manner

FROM my worthy friend M.ʳ Nicol of the High school, Edin.ʳ: alluding to some temeraire conduct of mine in the political opinions of that day. ——

Dear Chrystlefs Bobie,

What is become of thee? Has the ~~glade~~ Devil flown off with thee, as the glade does with a bird? — If he should do so, there is little matter, if the reports concerning thy imprudence are true. — What concerns it thee whether the flousy Dumfriesian fiddlers play Ça ira, or God save the king? {Suppose you had *an aversion* *to him*, you *could* *not*, as a gentleman, wish God to use him worse than he has done. —— The infliction of Ideocy is no sign of Friendship or Love; & I am sure, damnation is a matter far beyond your wishes or ideas.} But reports of this kind are only the insidious suggestions of ill-minded pirssons; for your good sense will ever point out to you, as well as to me, a bright model of political conduct, who flou-rished in the victorious reign of Queen Anne viz. the vicar of Bray, who during the convulsions of Great Britain, which were without any former example

example, saw eight reigns, in perfect security; because he remembered that precept of the <u>sensible</u>, <u>shrewd</u>, <u>temporising</u> Apostle — "We ought not to resist the Higher Powers". —

You will think I have gotten a pension from Government;. but I assure you, no such thing has been offered me. — In this respect, my vanity prompts me to say, they have not been so <u>wise</u> as I would have wished them; for I think their Honors have employ as impotent scribblers. ————

"Enough of Politics. — What is become of Mr. Burns & the dear bairns? How is my Willie? Tell her, though I do not write often, my best wishes shall ever attend her & the family. — My wife, who is in a high devotional fit this evening, wishes that she & her children may be reckoned the favorites of the Lord — and numbered with the Elect. — She indeed leaves your Honor & Me to shift for ourselves; as, as far as she can judge from the criteria laid down in Guthrie's trial of a saving interest, that both you & I are stamped with marks of Reproba-bation. ——————→

May

May all the curses from the beginning of Genesis to the end of Revelation, light, materially & effectually, on thy enemies; & may all the blessings of the Covenant be eminently exemplified in thy person, to the glory of a forgiving Deity!

Here, or elsewhere, I am always thine sincerely

Will:^m Nicol

Edin:^r 10th Feb:^{ry} -93}

As my friend Nicol, though one of the worthiest, &
positively the cleverest fellow I ever knew, yet no
man, in his humours, having gone greater lengths in
imprudence, unholiness, &c. than he; I wrote
him as follows. —

130

O thou, wisest among the Wise, meridian blaze of
Prudence, full-moon of Discretion, & Chief of many
Counsellors! —How infinitely is thy puddle-headed,
rattle-headed, wrong-headed, round-headed slave indebted
to thy supereminent goodness, that from the luminous
path of thy own right-lined rectitude, thou lookest
down benignly down on an erring Wretch, of whom
the zig-zag wanderings defy all the powers of
Calculation, from the simple copulation of Units up
to the hidden mystery of Fluxions! May one
feeble ray of that light of wisdom which darts
from thy sensorium, straight as the arrow of Jove
against the head of the Unrighteous, & bright
as the meteor of inspiration descending on the holy
&

undefiled Priesthood—may it be my portion; so that may be less unworthy of the face & favour of that other of Proverbs & master of Maxims, that antipode of Folly & magnet among the Sages, the wise & witty Willie Nicol! Amen! Amen! Yea, so be it!!!

For me, I am a beast, a reptile, & know nothing.— From the cave of my ignorance, amid the fogs of my dullness & pestilential fumes of my political heresies, I look up to thee, as doth a toad through the iron-barred lucarne of a pestiferous dungeon to the cloudless glory of a summer sun!—Sorely sighing in bitterness of soul, I say, when shall my name be the quotation of the Wise, & my countenance be the delight of the Godly, like the illustrious lord of ‡Laggan's many hills?—As for him, his works are perfect: never did the pen of Calumny blur the fair page of his reputation, nor the bolt of Hatred fly at his dwelling.—At his approach is the standing up of men, even the Chief & the Ruler; & before his presence the frail

a small estate of his—

                                    form

form of lovely Woman, humbly awaiting his pleasure, is extended on the dust. — Thou mirror of purity, when shall the elfine lamp of my glimmerous understanding, purged from sensual appetites & gross desires, shine like the constellation of thy intellectual powers. As for thee, thy thoughts are pure, & thy lips are holy. — Never did the unhallowed breath of the power of darkness & the pleasures of darkness, pollute the sacred flame of thy sky-descended, & heavenward bound desires: never did the vapours of impurity stain the unclouded serene of thy cerulean imagination. —— O, that like thine were the tenor of my life, like thine the tenor of my conversation! Then should no friend fear for my strength, no enemy rejoice in my weakness! Then should I lie down, & rise up, & none to make me afraid! ——

May thy pity & thy prayers be exercised for, —
O thou lamp of Wisdom & mirror of Morality!
Thy devoted slave—
R B

† The following was never scrolled, but is copied from the original letter. —

I suppose, my dear Madam, that by your neglecting to inform me of your arrival in + + + + + +, a circumstance which could not be indeed no occurrence relating to you can — you meant to leave me to guess & gather that a correspondence I once had the honor & felicity to enjoy, is to be no more. — — Alas, what heavy laden sounds are these — "no more!" — The wretch who has never tasted pleasure, has never known woe; but what drives the soul to madness, is the recollection of joys that are — "no more!" — But this is not language of the world. — They do not understand it. — But, come, ye children of Feeling & Sentiment; ye whose trembling bosom chords ach, to unutterable anguish, as recollection gushes on the heart! Ye who are capable of an attachment, keen as the arrow of Death, and strong as the vigour of Immortal Being — come! & your ears shall drink a tale — but hush! — I must not, can not tell it! Agony is in the recollection, & frenzy is in the recital! ————

Bro

But to leave these paths that lead to madness, I congratulate your friends, Madam, on your return; and I hope that the precious health which Miss + + + + + + + tells me is so much injured, is restored, or restoring. — There is a fatality attends Miss + — — + 's correspondence & mine. — + ‒ ╷ ╷

+

+

+ + + + + + + + + + + + + + + + + + + ╷ ╷

I present you a book: may I hope you will accept of it. — I dare say you have brought your books with you. — The fourth volume of + + + + + is published: I will also send it you. ——

. Shall I hear from you? — But first, hear me! — No cold language — no prudential documents. I despise Advice; & scorn Controul — If you are not to write such language, such sentiments, as you
know

now I shall wish, shall delight to receive; I conjure you, By wounded Pride! By ruined Peace! By frantic disappointed Passion! By all the many ills that constitute that sum of human woes— A broken heart! To me be silent for ever!!! — If you insult me with the unfeeling apothegms of cold-blooded Caution, Nay all the — but hold— a Fiend could not breathe a malevolent wish on the head of MY Angel! —

Mind my request! — If you send me a page baptised in the font of Sanctimonious Prudence — By Heaven, Earth & Hell, I will tear it into atoms! ———

Adieu! May all good things attend you!

R.B.

————————

I need scarcely remark that the foregoing was the fustian rant of enthusiastic youth. —

These letters appear to led to be scarcely the wers: he wrote

JC

To Miss Leſley Bailie of Mayville, inclosing a song I had composed on her. — 1793 —

Madam,

I have just put the last hand to the inclosed song; & I think that I may say of it, as Nature can of you — "There is a work of mine, finished in my "very finest style." —

Among your sighing swains, if there should be one whose ardent sentiment & ingenuous modesty fetter his powers of speech in your presence; with that look & attitude so native to your manner, & of all others the most bewitching —— Beauty listening to Compaſsion —— put my Ballad in the poor fellow's hand, just to give a little breathing to the fervour of his soul.. ——

I have some pretence, Madam, to make you the theme of my song, as you & I are two downright singularities in human nature. —— You will probably start at this aſsertion; but I believe it will be allowed that a woman exquisitely charming, without the least eming consciousness of it; & a Poet who never paid a compliment but where it was justly due; are two of the greatest rarities on earth. —

I have the honor to be — &c. —

To Miss Davies — inclosing a ballad —— 1791 or 92 or 89

Madam,

65

I understand that my very worthy neighbour, Mr
Riddell, has informed you that I have made you the subject
of some verses. — There is something in the idea of being
the burden of a ballad, that I do not think Job or Moses, though
such patterns of patience & meekness, could have resisted the
curiosity to know what that ballad was: & my worthy
friend, what I dare say he never intended, has done me a
mischief; & reduced me to the unfortunate alternative of
leaving your curiosity ungratified, or else disgusting you
with foolish verses, the unfinished production of a random
moment, & never meant to have met your ear. — I have
heard or read somewhere, of a gentleman, who had some
genius, much eccentricity, & very considerable dexterity
with his pencil. — In the accidental groupes of social
life into which one is thrown, whenever this gentleman
met with a Character in a more than ordinary degree
congenial to his soul, he used to steal a sketch of the
face, merely, he said, as a nota bene to point out the
agreeable

greeable recollection to his memory. — What this gentleman's
pencil was to him, is my Muse to me; & the inclosed verses
I do myself the honor to send you, are a memento & pretty of
the same kind. — It may be more owing to the fastidiousness
of my caprice than the delicacy of my taste, but I am so
often tired, disgusted & hurt with the insipidity, affectation
& pride of mankind, that when I meet with a person "after
my own heart," I positively feel what an orthodox Protestant
would call a species of idolatry, & which acts on my mind
like inspiration, & I can no more resist rhyming on the
impulse, than an Æolian harp can refuse its tones to
the streaming air. — A distich or two would be the consequence,
though the object of my fancy were grey-bearded, wrinkled
Age; but where my theme is Youth & Beauty, a young
Lady whose personal charms, wit & sentiment are
equally striking & unaffected, by Heavens! though I
had lived threescore years a married man, & threescore
years before I was a married man, my imagination
would hallow the very idea; & I am truly sorry that
the inclosed stanzas have done such poor justice to such
a subject —

         I have the honor &c. —